THE BIRDS
OF THE AIR

THE BIRDS
OF THE AIR

Parables of Loneliness and Unloneliness

DAVID DRAKE-BROCKMAN

"If you would learn more, seek information
from the birds of the air."
JOB, 12, 7

SEARCH PRESS
London and Tunbridge Wells

PAULIST PRESS
New York   Ramsey

First published 1982

In Great Britain by
Search Press Limited,
Wellwood, North Farm Road,
Tunbridge Wells, Kent TN2 3DR

In the United States by
Paulist Press,
545 Island Road,
Ramsey, N.J., 07446

ISBN (UK) 0 85532 445 7
ISBN (USA) 0 8091-0331-1
Library of Congress Catalog Card Number: 81-85168

Printed and bound in Great Britain
at The Pitman Press, Bath

TO

DOM CYPRIAN MARTIN,
O.S.B.

THE AASVOGEL

There was a good deal of circumstance about the preparations, as though they were setting out on the journey of life itself.

It was still dark when the crack of a whip was heard in the meadow below the bungalow and the oxen were roused and taken to the yard. A couple of men held lanterns while they were inspanned, amid much cheerful shouting and confusion, while others loaded the wagon. When all was ready they moved off. Either in the wagon or walking beside it were the farmer, his small son, a couple of other children staying with them, and eight or nine of the hands.

The ever-hopeful aasvogel had been woken by the whipcrack, and on hearing continued sounds of activity had climbed into the sky to see what was going on. Between the various noises and the feeble light of the lanterns he was able to make out what was happening, and when the cortège started off he resolved to accompany it.

By this time there was a certain amount of daylight. The yoked oxen ambled along the main track that led to the far-distant highway, their manner suggesting a comfortable private stroll rather than the traction of a heavy vehicle. Whenever they approached a gate one of the men walking would spurt ahead and open it, so the wagon kept moving at a constant speed. But they came at length to a gate which they didn't go through. Instead they turned off the track before it, and lumbered across country.

Soon they were in the bush. By now the sun was up and picking out the features of the landscape with exaggerated clarity. There were patches of scrub in otherwise open country, and there were long stretches more closely wooded – in places quite impenetrable. There were anthills frequently and waterholes occasionally. Everywhere grew the rough grey twisted gummy thorn trees. A bushbuck would hear them coming and crash into the undergrowth. A duiker would peer at them and then flee away behind the trees. A large tortoise would try to crouch down lower in the hole in the sand in which she was busy laying her eggs.

9

All morning the wagon went on without stopping. The guest children had not been up-country before, and excitedly pointed out to each other all the strange sights and happenings. When the sun was at its height they stopped for lunch, after which for half an hour the men rested while the children chased one another or tried to climb the anthills. Then they went on.

In the afternoon the gaiety had gone. The children were still interested in what was to be seen, but absorbed it silently. The others too only spoke from time to time, when the business in hand demanded it, and low and shortly. The wagon never stopped at all. There was something inexorable about its progress.

The sun went down and the world was filled with darkness, soft but complete. There was nothing to be seen. The only sounds were the creaking of the yokes, the clang of the iron tyres against stones, and the occasional laugh of a hyena. Time and place began to melt, and it felt as though they were floating nowhere in particular, as in a dream.

Suddenly there were lights ahead. The oxen plodded into a yard and stopped, and the children tumbled wearily out of the wagon. They had in fact returned to where they had started from those many hours before.

All day the aasvogel had flapped his way along above the wagon. He couldn't make out what it was all about. The party had travelled in a circle and got back to their starting point, having done very little on the way and achieved nothing at all. The whole thing seemed to him an entirely meaningless exploit.

(The aasvogel was an observant but not particularly philosophical bird. The idea of a perimeter inspection was not something that came into his consideration. But the farmer was satisfied that a good day's work had been done.)

THE ALBATROSS

For many days the albatross accompanied the ship. He was a big good-natured sort of fellow, and seemed to possess a kind of peace, for the beat of his wings was never hurried and his eye too was calm and wise and far-seeing. He was all on his own the whole time, but obviously not worried by that. If you had asked him doubtless he would have said: 'There's no loneliness in being alone if you want to be. If you don't want to be, that's when it may take strength. But the real killing loneliness is the sense of being left out of life or of whatever's going on.' The albatross seemed well enough adjusted, confident of being an integral part of life.

THE AUK

The great auk is extinct. Whatever others may feel about it, the great auks themselves no longer find it a matter of any concern whether they are extinct or not.

THE BABBLER

The babbler was an empirical bird, but eventually he learned the pitfall of empiricism, which is that experience is limited. It was Manzoni who wrote: 'To do good one must know what it is, and like everything else we can only know this by means of our own passions, our own judgments, our own ideas – which often don't amount to very much.'

THE BARN OWL

The barn owl sat awake in his hollow tree. He was working on a speech which he purposed to make at the next meeting of the birds' assembly. He was heavy-hearted, for he knew there would be trouble over this speech. He was going to take an unfashionable line on a certain much-debated question. The press would be able to make headlines by criticizing him, so the public would be against him. His friends too would be against him, in these days when the party line is paramount.

He was taking enormous pains over the precise phrasing of this speech, for he knew very well that people become animated frequently not so much by what you say as by what they decide you've said, however misunderstood or even misheard. – He was resigned to the fact that this would happen anyway, but still he wanted to take the utmost care to prevent it.

Why, knowing what he was in for, did he proceed with his intention? The answer was a kind of compulsion, a vocation almost, arising from truths which he considered to be more important than his own well-being. He was not without self-interest, he supposed, because if he made the speech, even if no one thereafter would have anything to do with him, he would be at peace with himself. He knew from past experience the terrible aloneness of universal unpopularity. But for him this isolation was as nothing compared with the sense of being cut off which would follow the failure on his part to do what he deemed himself called to do.

THE
BESPECTACLED OWL

(A nineteenth-century Oxford bird)

The owl sat there offering nothing but quiet sagacity.

There had been another bird, a bright and burning bird, who passed across the stage like a comet. This was the brilliant leader everyone craved. But circumstances arose and he found it good to move to other things. – Who should blame him?

The bespectacled owl, however, stayed where he was. In spite of his difficulties, in spite of the desertion of many of his friends, in spite of persecution by authorities, in spite of pressure from his more activist followers, in spite of the tragedies of his personal life, he still pursued his own quiet way. His wisdom was always available but he never sought to dominate. What such a lonely and devoted self-restraint may have cost him we cannot tell. What it achieved we can.

So, it was the owl who was significant, and not the comet. The comet defected but the owl persisted. The defection proved to be of little moment, but the persistence was of enormous importance; how enormous is evidently still largely unrecognized.

THE BITTERN

'Why does the bittern boom all day
    (And also half the night)?'
'Perchance to chase the gloom away,
    Perchance from simple fright.'

'Why does the bittern boom so long?
    Why does he boom so loud?'
'Perhaps his feelings are so strong.
    Perhaps he's very proud.'

'Why does the bittern boom at all?
    What does he think he gains?
Why can't he have a normal call
    In clear and dulcet strains?

'And does the bittern mourn a friend?
    Or celebrate a feast?'
'Perhaps you'll find that in the end
    It matters not the least.

'I think this conversation's turned
    Exceedingly absurd.
If you are really so concerned
    Why don't you ask the bird?'

THE BLACKBIRD

As always she called a diffident greeting when we passed.

Her old brown spotted coat was very worn, but she contrived to seem tidy and immaculately clean. Chatty, fussy in manner, she yet never unless asked to minded anyone's business but her own. Having a certain humble pride and a natural kindliness, she scorned to join in the gossip circles. She found herself much alone in consequence.

She kept in her nest a collection of holly berries which she had had for many years. These she would pass from claw to claw, finding they would give her a rhythm of prayer which was immensely helpful. From this came a whole rhythm of life.

She herself was only too aware that this was an aid and not an answer. There were more radical and more rowdy measures, but these it was simply not in her to adopt. She was content. Nevertheless, she was always glad of company.

THE BLOUWSIE

At one end of the street was the cathedral, standing in a little square of its own. It was out of place, a small conventional Victorian Gothic affair which would have made a fine and suitable parish church for a well-to-do suburb five thousand miles away.

The street itself was different, eminently of its own place. It was broad – very broad – and rather dusty; at least, it gave the impression of being dusty. All along each side was an unbroken row of low houses, stone, colour-washed but of nondescript colour. Each house had a single well-scrubbed step at the front door, and a brass bell-pull. Only the house nearest the cathedral on one side had neither step nor bell, for it was a shop – a very good bookshop for such a small town. Between the houses and the roadway were broad shallow pavements, and at the edges of these, casting their shade over much of the street, were jacaranda trees.

On one of these sat a blouwsie. He was a shaking and bedraggled creature, evidently not quite right in the head, and certainly exhibiting every sign of self-neglect. On the next tree a crowd of young birds of various kinds (and plenty not so young) were prancing up and down and chattering, complacent with the knowledge that they conformed to the standards of behaviour they had themselves set, secure in the assumption that to conform is the ultimate of life, whether it's conformity to loutishness, or to outlandishness, or to brutality, or even to an apparent flouting of conformity. Actually they were chanting

> 'Just look at the blouwsie;
> The blouwsie is lousy'.

Once the blouwsie had been a spruce young bird, full of eagerness for life. Then some tragedy had occurred (no one remembered what), and he had become abstracted. He no longer bothered about the things that seem so unimportant in the face of life's rawness. Other birds began to smile at him, instead of with friendliness, at first with pity and then with derision. He began to mumble to himself as he went about. Other birds tapped their temples. He ceased to care about himself altogether, and became an object to be avoided both from fear and from disgust. There seemed to be something of inevitability about his progress from the admirable to the despicable, and he never got round to perceiving that this inevitability was a delusion.

The world is made of vicious circles, and of even more vicious descending spirals.

THE BRAMBLING

The brambling had no mate. Sometimes he felt he was the only bird in the forest that had no mate. This involved him in two kinds of pretence. With birds who knew he had no mate he would pretend that he preferred it that way. But with strange birds he would often imply that he did have a mate. He would peer about as though looking for her. He would fly off with food as though to feed a family. He would decline invitations on the grounds that it was as much as his life was worth if he got home late, though in fact there was no one to care if he came home at all.

THE BUDGERIGAR

A budgerigar lay dying. Dying of a peculiarly painful and repellent disease.

Her loved ones were close by and going about their business. Her friends were thinking of her.

Her expression was of complete peace, even as the torment racked her.

THE BULBUL

While at the bungalow
The sad shades of valiant men and women
Converse and laugh politely
In the final dusk,
Alone in faded palaces
Where scorpion and cobra rule the dusty floor
And the crumbling roofs monotonously drip
The disinherited
Ponder their betrayal.

THE BULLFINCH

The thin snow mingles with the rotting leaves
And life itself is chilled.

Though four feet in the heartless clay your body fades
And much you knew is changed,
Oh, be not lonely in the unsonged night.

THE BUNTING

The bunting was an only child. What he could never get anybody to understand was that he liked being an only child, and liked being on his own. Everybody was for ever fussing round and saying they must find him someone to play with. But they didn't know what an agony of embarrassment it was for him when they found one. Two or three tried companions there were whom he did like to join forces with occasionally, but to be suddenly faced with a stranger produced just for the sake of it – oh, it was torture.

The bunting had an imagination and was able to people his world with all the friends and enemies he needed, far more congenial than real ones. He was an eagle, he was a lark, he was a swan, just as the fancy took him. Whatever adventures he wanted were his, without having to dilute them to suit a friend's conception. So long as he was alone there was always music in his ears.

THE BURGOMASTER

The day was perfect. The sky was so intensely blue as to seem unreal, the sea had just sufficient lazy movement to keep it alive rather than dull, the breeze was so light as to be unfelt but enough to take the edge off the sun's heat. There were only two creatures to be seen; one was a man and the other was a gull.

The man was one of some importance and renown in the world of men; he was both a man of letters and a man of affairs. At the present moment he was thoroughly enjoying a day off, lying on his back on the springy headland, indolently chewing a sandwich, and watching fascinated the movements of the bird.

The latter was a large snowy creature, a glaucous gull, known in some parts as a 'burgomaster'. He too was evidently rejoicing in the day, for he was soaring and swooping, making arcs against the sky so optically satisfying as to stupefy. A veritable artist in aerodynamic exhibitionism one would have said of him if it hadn't all seemed so innocent and carefree. To judge from the length of time he kept it up he could hardly fail to be enjoying himself.

At length the man got up with a sigh. He went back to his room and wrote verses and pamphlets musing on why men are unable to be as free as the birds, with no cares in the world and the wind and the sea for constant companions.

The bird too went home eventually. As he approached he could hear the screech of his mate above the hubbub of the colony: 'Where have you been all day, you good-for-nothing show-off! Here have I been working myself to the bone! Go and get some food for the young this instant. And when you come back you can mend the nest; it's collapsing again, thanks to your idleness!'

THE BURROWING OWL

In the graveyard at Waterbury Center
The tombstones stand in tidy rows,
Like the neat plots of the Sephardim
In more eclectic cemeteries, or
Like thin grey seasoned soldiers
Impassive through the rain.

Once when it rained like this
The Imjin burst its banks
And spread across the plain
Making each hillocked company an island.
At times each man seemed an island
Alone in a sea of unaccustomed thoughts
– Green Mountain Boys who'd come
To moot with curious dedication their philosophy.
Could it be this, –
Some vague idea to keep the Imjin's dirty aftermath
From their own bright hills?

After a day or two the flood went down
Leaving a squalid tidemark on the insipid earth.
Here all will be green tomorrow
And vetch and figwort lift unruffled heads.

THE
BUZZARD

Although I visited her often and always stayed a long time she
complained constantly that I neglected her. I couldn't go more
often, or stay longer, because there were so many in the same
position. Most of them were grateful for what little time one could
spare them, but not she. And she was such a bore.

But how lonely she must have been to be able to bring herself,
knowing she was a bore, to beg for more of my time.

THE
CANARY

A canary lay dying. She was not ill at all, just fading peacefully away after a long life.

She was entirely on her own, except for one old bird in the adjoining cage who took no notice of her.

In her eye was a look of terror.

THE
CARDINAL

The cardinal, the protonotary, and the friar, agreed to preach on the same text from the day's epistle: Ephesians, ch.4, v.25. The cardinal spoke as follows:

'We are members one of another'. This is both a statement of fact and a Christian command. As a statement of fact it is true in several senses. It's true in the obvious sense that those of us who live in any one place are members of a community, and there is a limit to the extent to which we can indulge our individual behaviour without disturbing or interfering with our neighbours. It's true in the sense that some trivial action on the part of an individual person the other side of the world could bring about, for instance, a strike which causes an increase in the price of, say, sugar, which affects us all. It's true in the sense that everyone's work, paid or unpaid, whether it's public service, or in a shop, running a house and family, whatever it is, is part of the fabric of society; without the individual threads there is no fabric. It's true in the sense that anything we say to someone else may affect his relations with a third person. Above all it's true in the sense that none of us can exist without relationships. And I think perhaps it's true to say that loneliness is the cruellest of all forms of suffering.

'Now Paul was not just stating these things, but exhorting his readers, as Christians, to take them a stage further. Loving our neighbour is not merely a matter of regulating our behaviour so as, rather negatively, not to do him any harm. Rather it's a matter of finding out what we can do positively for him. It's a matter of considering not just whether the immediate consequences of our actions will be harmful to anyone, but the long-term consequences too. It's a matter of giving a share of ourselves to society. And it's a matter of realising that loneliness is a terrible anomaly in a Christian community.'

THE CATBIRD

'Now stills the air,
Now falls the night,
Now frights my heart despairing of your love.'
– And is it true you've gone,
Selling the key to our castillo,
Like Tarpeia,
For a bangle? –

THE CHOUGH

They had thought that they would be able to carry on just the same without the chough that had gone away, but it was not so.

When he was with them they had met often, and the meetings had been fruitful for them all. The conversation had been brilliant; wit had darted from one to another, caught and passed on, singing like silver. Ideas blossomed and were often lost through their sheer abundance. Inspiration became the air they breathed.

And then he had announced that he was leaving the country for good. It was sad that one of the group should leave it, but there seemed no reason why it should be any more than that. They had arranged to go on meeting in the same way and to talk about the same things, to share their evenings and their thoughts as they had always done.

But it soon was clear that virtue had gone with the chough that went away. Laughter was seldom heard and rather desperate. Ideas were trivial, not worth pursuing. The meetings were dull, and became less frequent.

Searching to find a reason, they realized that they had never been a group on their own, had no close relationships with one another, but had been held together by their common individual friendship with the chough that had gone away. It was he who had been the mainspring of their creativeness.

And so they tried to personify his memory, and insisted that he was with them whenever they came together. But it didn't work, the quality of their genius belied them. There was a franticness about the whole enterprise. It was too contrived, and in the end they went their individual ways. A God can be present in the abstract, but not, it seems, the most brilliant of choughs.

THE
COCK-OF-THE-ROCK

There was chaos and corruption on the rock, and the burly little red bird saw himself as the one to sort it out. – He did sort it out, promptly and very effectively, and everyone looked forward to a new order of things.

But the trouble was that though he had the personality to dominate he didn't have the intelligence to direct. Things very soon began to go wrong. In order to distract attention from himself and from these failures he began to produce scapegoats, first other species then other members of his own kind. These were either killed or expelled, and his people were satisfied for the time being by such offerings. But as the victims had for the most part been fairly useful members of society, in the long run it merely made things worse. By crisis after crisis the régime moved towards disaster.

If it had been possible to ignore the terror and unhappiness that were so widespread, the most interesting thing about the whole business was the gradual change in the cock-of-the-rock's own character. He had been a bluff, jovial individual, quite secure in his relationship with his fellows, well-liked and trusted, honest and without ambition. – His motive in seizing power was a genuine concern for the state of affairs existing and an equally genuine conviction that he was the one who could right matters. But once having accepted responsibility he became obsessed with the idea that only he was capable of seeing straight, and that he must for the sake of all concerned cling to power at any cost. He had been a kind and gentle individual; now his conscience rapidly withered before the assumed necessity of performing more and more terrible deeds.

It seemed to boil down really to the isolation created inevitably by the nature of his office in those circumstances. He had been a gregarious sort of character; now he was so frighteningly alone.

THE
CORMORANT

Mist came down with the dusk. It was not a pervasive all-over sort of mist, nor was it a low mist hovering just above the sea. Rather it was a thick layer of mist lying at a certain level in the air, so that the great white castle at the top of the hill seemed to be floating on it like some majestic and impregnable warship, while the village perched precariously on the steep lower slopes of the hill was entirely below it.

In this village lights were appearing one by one. Presently one such light detached itself and moved across the water. It became apparent that this was a flare burning in the bows of a fishing boat. The outline of the craft curved down in a flattened arc from its high prow almost to the waterline at the stern. This pleasing line was broken in three places: by the basket in the bows containing the burning twigs, by a cormorant perched on the gunwale close to it, and by the rather bent figure of a man sitting in the stern.

There were several islands dotted about the entrance to the bay, and many others disappearing into the distance in the open sea beyond. The silhouettes of these, black against the fiery sky whence the sun had just gone down, made a lurid picture. The water was as smooth and heavy as oil; it seemed almost sacrilege to spoil its marble-like surface by dipping a paddle into it. Apart from the faint stir of bubbles made by the paddle, and the creak of wood, there was no sound.

The fisherman was very old. His face was lined with a thousand wrinkles, his wispy hair grey and thin, his eyes almost closed. He no longer fished commercially, but simply for his own food, which is why he only had one bird. This creature, like all of its kind so employed, had a line attached to one leg and a leather choker round the base of its throat.

Arrived at the place it seemed good to him to fish, the man pushed the bird off the boat into the water. It dived, and presently reappeared, struggling back on to the boat. Prevented by the choker from swallowing the fish it had caught, it opened its beak waiting for the fisherman to pull the fish from its throat and throw them into the basket in the middle of the boat. The patient faces of the pair of them were lit gaudily by the burning flare.

Twice more the bird dived, returned, and gave up its catch. But the last time, as he bent forward to reach into the bird's gullet the fisherman was taken by some kind of seizure. After trying in vain to shake it off, or to turn the boat for shore, or both, he picked up his knife and managed to cut both the line and the choker, so that the bird was free.

The tide took the boat slowly over the bay. The old man lay dead in the bottom. The cormorant continued to dive and reappear, and, since there was no one to take them, itself threw up the fish into the basket.

THE CRAKE

The crake was badly crippled – had been for years. She was no hypochondriac. The disease was real enough, for you could see that her legs were badly bent and her toes twisted out of joint. She was also very lonely. Eventually we busybodies managed to manoeuvre her into a crowd of friends – real friends, a group to which she was able to feel she belonged. That took care of her loneliness. The extraordinary thing was that her legs and toes began to straighten out, and she was soon able to get about again.

THE CRANE

Precise, unhurried, dignified,
The formal measure of our formlessness,
Presenting patterns that we wish confused
And fine uncertainties that we deplore.
We roll among the rotting swedes
And dream our dreams
Of old well-mannered rose gardens
And the exciting wilderness beyond,
And that perhaps is all.
Or perhaps it is too much,
And the mind may fail sometimes
To carry such a burdened soul.
Life is a minuet no longer.

THE CUCKOO

I can remember that there were others in the nest at one time. I don't know what happened to them. I can recollect a sort of frenzy. And after that, and all the time I can remember clearly, I was on my own in the nest. I often wished for someone else, – to be able to feel there were others near. And all the time I couldn't help a guilty feeling it was my fault the others had disappeared. But I couldn't piece anything together.

I was looked after by foster parents. They were kind little things, and very good to me. It must have been hard work for them to feed me, because I soon became much bigger than they; but they were quite devoted, and never left me wanting. Yet all the time I could never avoid the suspicion that they really hated me, that they thought I didn't belong and was in some way to blame for a catastrophe, that they only persevered through a sort of religious sense of duty. It was very uncomfortable.

THE CURLEW

The storm picked up the curlew as though he were no more than a dry leaf. It whirled him through circles in every plane and battered him from one wind eddy to another. It seemed to go on for many hours, but mercifully he lost consciousness in the end.

When he awoke the first thing he was aware of was pain in both wings. He didn't move for a long time. When he did, it was to try his wings gently; there was agony, but no movement. Again he kept still for a long time, until the pain had subsided to its previous level. Then he thought to try if his legs also were broken, but they weren't.

Carefully he began to explore his surroundings. He discovered that the storm must have stuffed him into a crack between two rocks, and when he emerged from the crack he found himself close to the top of a rough hill. By waddling round the back of the rocks and struggling up the slope he reached the top of the hill and could see in every direction.

He was on an island, and there was no other island in sight. He could tell from the climate and from the vegetation of the island, which were quite different from those of his homeland, that the storm had carried him a very long way indeed. There was no trace at all of any bird or animal life.

The curlew was marooned, alone, hundreds of miles from help, and with both wings broken. The realization of this crept up on him gradually. When it did, he shrank into a numbness of fear and helplessness and lostness. He tottered back to his crack in the rocks and lay there as though awaiting death.

But in time the numbness passed and a more hopeful mood took hold of him. He began to feel that perhaps rescue might come, or perhaps he could escape if he had the patience to wait till his wings healed and in the meantime kept himself as fit as possible. Food and shelter were the prime necessities. Shelter of a kind he had, but he needed something more secure and comfortable and nearer the shore. But food, that was the first thing. Now it was determination that took and excited him.

He found a plentiful food supply, even if it wasn't what he was used to. And he gradually built himself a fine nest. All the time he looked on these as temporary measures, just for the duration of his stay on the island, which wouldn't be long.

However, no craft or creature of any kind ever came within view. And his wings, though they mended in time, did so in such a way that they would never again be usable. But he ceased to mind. He came to find a great satisfaction in his life on the island, a fulfilment. He could relax there in a way he never could have elsewhere, for there was no one to bother about, no day-to-day worries, no predators, no possibility of human development to disturb the peace, no competition for food and nesting sites, just endless peace. After all, rescue was something to be dreaded.

It did happen after a year or two that he felt dissatisfied for a while. A restlessness took hold of him, a boredom with the lack of facilities to some extent, but much more a vague feeling that he wasn't achieving anything. – Very likely he wouldn't have been achieving any more if he'd been with others of his kind, but at least he would have been having the opportunity.

This phase passed, though, and he was left with a resignation, a quiet acceptance of his lot, which sustained him to the end of his days.

THE
DABCHICK

There can be a loneliness of dying, but not a loneliness of death. Whether one's view of the hereafter tends to paradise or to oblivion, there is no need to pity the dead. The sadness of death consists only in the loneliness of those who are left.

THE
DEMOISELLE

An immense area of the palace grounds consisted of various formal gardens side by side, each square in shape. If one could have seen it from the air it would have looked like a chess board, only instead of alternate colours the squares contained each a different pattern, formed by the hedges, rose bushes, ponds, statues, and other ornaments used to compose the pictures in that horticultural gallery.

Although they were free to roam, one square in particular was the abode of the demoiselle cranes. Here you would always find them, picking their way fastidiously about, as though conscious of their high function and destiny, as though in time to some unheard pavane. Never hurried, never flustered, they certainly expected other beings to move out of their way in that domain. A brief stare, the acme of superciliousness, was the most they would accord to strangers.

The adjoining square was the garden set aside for the recreation of the maids of honour from the court. Here one would often see

Lancret pictures come to life, as the young girls released the energy pent up by the decorum of the court. Unlike the birds, the maids if they came on a stranger would smile and gently disappear. Like the birds, they were free to come and go but simply stayed.

One might wonder why birds so lovely and so spirited as the demoiselles chose to remain as it were in a showcase: a place of comfort and magnificence but none the less a cage, though it had no bars. One gathers it was partly a sense of the rightness of appointed order, and partly a security of comradeship: – who knows who one's fellows would be in the world outside?

THE DIPPER

The birds were strolling in their hundreds. Only the dipper walked alone. None had invited him to walk with them. He could have attached himself to a group, or himself suggested one. But he might have been snubbed. It was too great a risk.

THE
DIVER

There is a certain lake a couple of hundred miles north of here, very secluded, not close to any track. It is not a large lake, scarcely more than half a mile across. Trees grow right to the water's edge, big ones and a thick undergrowth of young ones, hemlocks, rowans, maples, and choke-cherries. Close to one side of the lake is a small clearing and a cabin; the cabin is often not used from one year to the next, and the clearing disappears until someone turns up and once again reclaims it. In one corner of the lake is a small sleeve-shaped bay. It was here one year that a diver who had got separated from his kind set up his home.

One afternoon as the diver was returning from a flight he noticed that part of the clearing had been newly cultivated. But he could see no sign of life. Having landed on his little inlet he paddled down to the mouth of it and hid himself in the reeds. All evening he waited there observing the cabin, but saw nothing. The next day again he stationed himself where he could see the cabin, but although there seemed at one time to be smoke coming from the chimney he saw nobody. In the evening he flew high above the lake and found that the cleared area had been enlarged.

For several days he kept a careful watch on the hut and its surroundings. Although the clearing grew day by day he never caught sight of a human. Eventually he lost interest and resumed his normal life. One evening he was coming in to land, flying rather low over the lake, when he suddenly became aware of a canoe on the water below him. There was a man in the canoe. He obviously heard the beat of the diver's wings, for he turned to look and then reached for a shotgun. The diver in alarm darted for home and arrived safely. He heard no shot, but couldn't swear there wasn't one.

That human being was a bit of a ruffian, who respected neither man nor beast. He had got into trouble in the city, and now aimed to lie low in this remote spot until the affair had blown over. He had spent many days clearing and planting the patch behind the cabin. Having completed that job he was able to go fishing. He was engaged in this when he heard the sound of a large bird approaching, and picked up his gun, which he always had lying handy. He had a good view of the bird as it flew low over him and away, but for some reason which he could never understand he didn't pull the trigger.

The diver resumed his cautious and curious observations of the man. Normally man was a creature he would take good care to avoid. But in his present isolation he was prepared to take an interest in any kind of being. However, he didn't forget the gun, and he took care to remain out of sight. In time he got bolder, and would go quite close to the cabin or the canoe, always remaining in the cover of the reeds.

The man too, for his part, though he'd never before shown much interest in any creature other than himself, began to look on the diver with a sort of fellow-feeling. He was used to companionship, rough and little good though it may have been, and in this place the diver seemed to be all the possible companion there was. Often he caught sight of him peering from the reeds, and after the first couple of times never dreamed of using his gun.

It was a good many weeks before they made real contact, but they did in the end.

THE
DODO

The dodo is dead. Long may he flourish.

The deadness of the dodo is proverbial. He is as dead as any doornail (or, as Dickens prefers it, any coffin-nail). Yet everyone knows all about the dodo. He is a household word. Your ordinary common-or-garden run-of-the-mill man-in-the-street wouldn't know a three-stringed bar-winged green-tailed yellow-eyed lesser level-headed shrieker if he saw one. But he'd know a dodo all right.

THE
DOMINICAN

The dominican cardinal is a handsome bird from South America. At that moment, however, he was worried. He felt himself to be extremely isolated. He was conscious that as the council proceeded the others were becoming more and more suspicious of him. The conservatives thought him a progressive, the radicals thought he was really a soft-soaping diehard, and the liberals didn't trust him either way. The truth is that he was simply perplexed. How should he vote? He knew the measure was inevitable, he knew it was beyond question right, but it was his conviction that in the long run it would prove a mistake. Yet however bad it might turn out to be, since it was right and couldn't be avoided would it be either useful or ethical to impede it? On the other hand, wouldn't it be pure expediency to bow to the inevitable, even if it was also right? It seemed to him that they were bound to lose either way. It just wasn't possible to go on in the old way, yet the new would make such a radical difference as to render it questionable whether it was worth going on at all.

He almost cursed his lack of partisanship. At the beginning there had been room for moderate thinking, but as opinions hardened only extremists could get a following. It seems, he thought, that those able to see both sides of a question attract more often the execration than the admiration of both sides.

THE DOWITCHER

The dowitcher was accused of cheating. It was in fact an unjust accusation. There was no reason why he would have cheated, and there was no evidence that he had. It was simply that he had done rather better than usual. Such is the addiction of some creatures to the idea of natural regularity that when something occurs a little out of the regular it is assumed to be unnatural.

Anyone the dowitcher tried to speak to turned away without answering. Whenever a fault was found or a misdemeanour committed the dowitcher was automatically saddled with it until it should become indisputably clear that someone else was to blame. No one would have anything to do with him. Wherever he went he heard a whispered chorus of 'cheat'.

There was no question of his being able to establish his innocence, nor was there any possibility of this coming to light. There was nothing which could come to light, no evidence either way. It was simply a matter of enduring the unpleasantness until the episode should be forgotten.

THE EAGLE

No more
     Shall we meet here, my brother.

Early
     In the morning I go.

Sometimes
     We shall hear of each other.

Always
     That I loved you you'll know.

Vale,
     May the Gods give you keeping.

Vale,
     Till our fates bring us home.

Vale,
     Till the whirlwinds are reaping.

Vale,
     Till we meet then in Rome.

THE FLAMINGO

There was the feeling of a breeze in the air – not an actual breeze, just a barely perceptible lessening of hopelessness after days and days of the flat itching heat. There was no sound, no hint of movement, from the reeds along the lakeshore, yet one could swear they were living plants again and not just integral parts of the general lifeless landscape.

From out of the reeds the head of a flamingo sardonically appeared. After glancing about with weary uninterest it moved forward, followed by the whole cynical neck and body and legs of the bird. Once clear of the reeds the various parts became more apparently the coherent whole of a bird, rather than so many pieces left behind in the swelter. But it was a bird compounded strangely of innocence and disillusion. The implacable sun cared nothing for his dreams.

If we were to have entered into his mind we should have discovered a devouring unhappiness, clinging around the mythical pianist he was in love with. It wasn't that he was lonely without her; it was that he couldn't bear the thought of how lonely she must be without him. She must be, he considered, alternately playing elegiac melodies of her own composition and strolling with tortured eyes the streets and woods of her inhabiting, wistfully smoking, listlessly longing. Was it the heat that prevented their being together?

The cardinal, the protonotary, and the friar, agreed to preach on the same text from the day's epistle: Ephesians, ch.4, v.25. The friar spoke as follows:

"'We are members one of another.' This great truth is also expressed in Donne's famous dictum, almost a proverb by now, "No man is an island". The point is that no person, except obviously a hermit or a castaway, does or can live in complete isolation. Even if someone deliberately sets out to be a recluse, he has to get food from somewhere, which means he has to talk to somebody, so here is the beginning of at least one relationship. Life is a matter of relationships, and all our relationships affect one another. The deeper and wider our relationships are the fuller our own lives, and the greater understanding we are likely to have of people's problems, both immediate and remote. And that is why in any community the basis of a real community life is the fact of everybody's taking the trouble to get to know everybody else as well as possible.

'The result of having too few relationships is loneliness – the immediate result, that is – the long-term result often is a twisted mind, an over-developed imagination, a grudge against society, and so on, and the frequent outcome of those things is crime. People who are alone in a strange city are very often extremely lonely after working hours, living in a bed-sitter perhaps and never seeing their neighbours. The tragedy is that in a big city people like that are probably invisible to whatever of a community there is, and any initiative towards the acquiring of relationships has got to come from themselves.

'But there are of course people whose loneliness is the result of an aloneness which has been suddenly thrust on them. These are mostly older people, perhaps widows or widowers, or maiden ladies who have lost a sister, who live alone and who can't go out. Relatives who live at a distance come when they can; good neighbours pop in perhaps several times a day; what one might call professional visitors come from time to time. All this is a great help and sometimes succeeds in dispelling the loneliness entirely, but not always. Sometimes those concerned are obstinate and won't move though offered a share in someone else's house – but who should blame them if they're reluctant to leave the home in which, perhaps, they've spent most of their lives? This sort of loneliness remains a very great problem.

'In the matter of the lonely, the Christian is to welcome the stranger and to visit the alone (and also to be visited by him if he is mobile). Also, being members one of another, we should know one another and understand one another. We should rejoice in one another's good fortunes and help to bear one another's bad fortunes. We should take a hurt to the community as a hurt to ourselves, and an achievement by an individual as an achievement by the community whose love it was that influenced and formed the character of the individual. And each of us as individuals should listen to other members of the community and hear what they have to tell us about ourselves, because it's quite certain that we all have blind spots, and our friends, if we're prepared to listen to them, can help us to see what we perhaps are not able to see. And we should do the same for them. All this is what it means to be members one of another.'

THE FRIGATE BIRD

The frigate bird was happily mated and a leading light of the community. Then one day he went away to sea. He was away for many months, all the time looking forward to getting home again. When he did return he was given a warm welcome by all concerned, who were really glad to see him.

But he found that there was no longer room for him in the life he had left and hoped to resume. While he had been away life had gone on without him, and a pattern had emerged for his family and friends which didn't include him. Now he was surplus to the scheme of things, a disruption. The place he had filled had been overgrown, rather as the holes and trenches and castles which people make on the beach are smoothed over by the returning tide.

THE FULMAR

The fulmar was an unfortunate bird, in that she condemned herself to life on a spiral. Being lonely she joined every conceivable organization and activity; being aggressive and sure of her own opinions she tended to dominate; having dominated she found herself unpopular, and was sensitive enough thus to become lonely all over again. After a while she ran out of groups to join. In the end she found some kind of social life by assiduously courting visitors.

THE GAMECOCK

The gamecock was well known as the bravest soldier in the army. Any attack, and he was there first, cheering on those beside him. Any wounded to be brought in under fire, it was he who would do it. A patrol to go out, it was he who would lead it, to deeds of undreamed-of daring. Hand-to-hand fighting, it was he who would bear the brunt of it. Steady firing, he would expose himself cheerfully to the bullets in order to inspire the rest. When the troops were tired and wet and dispirited, and moving up into action once again instead of back to a scheduled rest, it was he who would start them singing.

One dark night the platoon was occupying an inconveniently large hill. There had been many casualties. There were not enough soldiers to go round, and the standing patrols had to consist of one instead of two or three. The gamecock found himself alone on a little spur. He could neither see nor hear his fellows. During the night there was plenty of activity but no action; not a shot was fired, not a shout was uttered, but there was a constant rustling as of people creeping, and the occasional rattle of a dislodged stone.

In the morning the gamecock's body was found at his post. There was not a mark on him. His heart had stopped, apparently from fright.

THE GANNET

A superficial observer watching some gannets diving thought they were a strange sect devoted to a kind of Russian roulette, so suicidal did their dives appear.

As a matter of fact some gannets are associated with that laudable society which aims to help those who contemplate suicide. I once heard a group of gannets debating the whole question.

The first quoted Nietzsche's opinion that we might have a right to take away a being's life but not his death. 'Es gibt ein Recht, wonach wir einem Menschen das Leben nehmen, aber keines, wonach wir ihm das Sterben nehmen: dies ist nur Grausamkeit.' In other words, if someone finds life insupportable it is the nadir of cruelty to force him to go on enduring it.

The second admitted that this was so with those who knew what they were doing and were determined to end their lives. And he mentioned the case of Captain Oates, which was a suicide entirely selfless carried out in an aloneness that was without loneliness. But, he said, the high proportion of unsuccessful suicide attempts made by people who were quite competent enough to do it successfully if they wanted to suggests that they really in their heart-of-hearts don't.

The third said that in the course of his work he had met many who were only too anxious to be talked out of suicide. What most of them were suffering from was an unbearable loneliness. However many and intimate friends we have there are some problems which can neither be shared with them nor supported alone.

The fourth said we have no right to condemn suicides; the morality of the matter is an issue solely between them and God. But the fact that someone can be so unhappy as to contemplate action so drastic is something which must concern us. Sometimes such people are crying out to us for help, and this is extremely hard for us to recognize. Sometimes, he said, he was appalled at the extent to which, by being preoccupied with his own vanities, he'd failed to notice that people were hiding a deep trouble.

THE GERFALCON

The first blown hint of snow has fallen
And the tribes go back to their villages.
For want of war our young men turn to crime,
Or heed the singing over the desert
Which calls them south and west
To where the muslin'd women of ease
Float in their scented gardens
In the cities of Turkestan.

But when the moon goes up on their unused limbs
And camel-pads across the heated sky
They shall hear the sigh of our horses at the picket

As it quivers through the dawn
And return in the hard seat of adventure
Over the joyful plain.

THE GOLDENEYE

They caught my eye right away, before the ship had even sailed. They were standing in the foyer, both very excited, obviously brother and sister, he in his late forties and she a dozen years younger. He was doing all the talking, rather loudly, making plans, discussing possibilities, and she was acquiescing willingly enough. A pleasant couple they seemed, close to each other but shyly remote from others – though far from unfriendly.

I saw them several times the first few days about the decks and public rooms, always together and rather wide-eyed. It looked as though this trip was an unaccustomed treat and they were eager to enjoy it to the full. But this was the naive and attractive joy of the unsated, not that determination to get the utmost for their money which characterises some cruise passengers.

After a couple of days the seating arrangement at our table was altered slightly, and I now found myself looking straight at the backs of the brother and sister. To start with they talked only to each other, though they would smile and reply politely if addressed; it was shyness, not ill-manners. But gradually the girl grew into the way of talking to the others, and eventually one conversation included the whole table. The brother, however, never joined in this general talk; any remark he made was addressed to his sister. The way he sat there looked suspiciously like sulking, but you never know.

What they did in the ports I can't say; probably they went on the tours; I never saw either of them ashore until the very last port.

While strolling across an open space I came across the brother, slovenly dressed and moodily turning this way and that, waiting for the museum to open. He was extremely dejected, distraught even, and looked years older. When I greeted him it took him several seconds to recognize me, and then he replied 'Oh hullo' in the dullest voice. I wanted to ask where his sister was, but thought better of it.

After the voyage I speculated a good deal on the result of it for those two. I'm afraid the whole thing was a cruel disappointment to him, but I hope that she at any rate found the door opened to new relationships.

THE GOLDFINCH

The goldfinch was the most generous and charitable bird in the entire aviary. Any collections being made, any good works being done, the goldfinch was the first to be applied to. 'Only too glad to help you', she would say, or: 'They need help so badly', and 'you' or 'they' would go away with good measure.

And yet the goldfinch didn't seem to be altogether a member of the community. In spite of the fact that everyone knew her and asked for her support she always seemed to be somehow out of things. She herself felt this and wondered why it was, for she would have liked to have been accepted.

Then one day when a certain project was being mooted she was heard to say that 'we' would have to do something about it. From then on she was in.

45

THE GOOSANDER

Nathaniel Flon, the cleric don,
    Adorned his Oxbrick study;
Green was his eye, his forehead high,
    Complexion somewhat muddy.
The air with 'Rave' (his after-shave)
    Reeked like Macgillicuddy.

While feckless flies before his eyes
    Were cutting dizzy capers,
The Reverend Nat sat staring at
    Examination papers,
Which ordinands from many lands
    Had entered – foolish japers.

'Oh, use your loaf, you silly ὡφ!'
    He wrote in great big letters.
'How dare you write a thing so slight
    And send it to your betters?'
– Useless. You see, his words can't be
    Deciphered by the getters.

He hurled his pen across the den
    And said in words so pretty
'I can but do *per diem* two;
    It's really such a pity.
But this must be, since they need me
    On many a committee.

'If only I were not so high
    In public estimation,
My life would be a lot more free
    And I'd have less vexation.'
– In actual fact this busy act
    Was nothing but frustration.

Though others' views he'd soon abuse
    In learned disputation,

Theology was not the key
    That wound his excitation;
Instead it was, I fear, because
    He lived in isolation.

THE GOOSE

Afterwards I waited for you
But you didn't come.
The next day was Sunday and the sun shone
Making of the lampposts on the Lombardsbrücke
Shadows like fools' wands on the water.
I wandered here and there among the crowd ...
They all had faces but none of them was yours,
And since the sun went on shining all the week
Eventually I forgot to look.

THE GOSHAWK

I can no longer outstare the sun.

I
Who was Uriel's daughter
Golden Infanta
Playmate of the dawn
Skulk in the damp and cobwebbed ruins
Of long-forgotten abbeys
With the throbbing fungus for a pillow
And nettles to shade my unsouled eyes.

The secret shouting of the windy night
No longer is romantic cavalry
Galloping endlessly over the hills
To mysterious victories and a gaudy death
But a wail of unliberated souls
Condemned to some interminable penance
In these thunder-gathering valleys.

And as the aconite beneath the ivied dusk
Folds the thin petals of its once Trojan animus
I
Inadequately try to hold my senses
That flee
In terror
From the pastimes of the gods.

THE GRASSWARBLER

The grasswarbler was in didactic mood. He said:

'It seems to me that grass is in some ways remarkably like birds or people. There are all sorts, tall and short, coarse and fine, sturdy and willowy. There are feathery grasses, furry ones, silky ones, prickly ones, knobbly ones – and plain ordinary nondescript ones. Some grasses grow on mountains, some on sand dunes, some in marshes, some in sophisticated lawns. In meadows and by the roadside you can see dozens of species of grass growing all intermingled with one another.

'I think there is a great deal we can learn from grass. You see, grass is always there – and flourishing. A violent storm can flatten grass, but it's very soon standing upright again. A fire can burn off all the vegetation; the grass is the first thing to reappear, little bright shots of green among the black. You can cut grass, shave it off almost level with the ground if you want; in a few days it's just as long as it was before. You can put paving stones on top of grass, but it will push its way up between them. You can pull it up by the roots, but it will leave its seed behind. Weedkiller will destroy it for a time, but it will come back in due course. You just can't win against grass.

'But there is one important difference between grass and people. Grass has this resilience, this capacity for recovery and regrowth, naturally; it does it automatically; it doesn't know any other way. Grass doesn't have a soul. We have souls, and we have wills. We too can recover from the disasters that happen to us, from all the blows both large and small, both personal and communal, which may come our way. But we don't do it automatically, and so there is always the danger that we may not do it at all. The key to it is trust, utter reliance.

'There is one other thing about grass. You never see a *single* blade of it. You may indeed see an isolated clump of it pushing through asphalt hundreds of metres from any other grass. But that clump is strong and at one. No blade is ever left on its own.'

THE GREBE

Summer ended suddenly one evening
With a windy storm that withered all the leaves
And left the air filled with a grey foreboding.
All through the storm and the long cold night that followed
The sedge lay motionless beneath the reeds,
Until the day broke
With the smell of some primeval burning
That is the special scent of autumn
And the sun like a red-hot penny
Hung in the morning.

A single joyous cry
Rang through the embers
Of that cremated summer.

THE GRIFFON

The imagination traditionally pictures the villains of the Passion narrative somewhat as three vile birds, representatives of Satan, plotting to bring about the destruction of God. But evil is much more subtle than that.

It was not only a matter of the time and the place and the circumstances. Surely loneliness too had something to do with it; for what seems to stand out is that these three were not particularly vile men, but lonely men. Two of the three suffered the loneliness of exalted position, while the third suffered the loneliness of being entirely amongst people with a different way of thought. Two of the three suffered the loneliness of being weak men caught up in events which called for strength. All suffered the loneliness of having to make a decision which they knew would be condemned.

Judas

The gospels do not tell us very much about Judas. The salient facts, as we all know, are that he was one of the Twelve, that he betrayed our Lord, was offered thirty pieces of silver for doing so, and then went and hanged himself – and accordingly he has become for all time the archetype of treachery. One other fact we know: by his surname, Iscariot, we are told that he came from a certain town in the south of Palestine; he was in fact a Judean, whereas all the others of the Twelve were, it would seem, Galileans, as was Jesus himself.

However, a strong clue to the reason for his conduct is given us in the story of the anointing at Bethany. Someone complained about the waste of money in using up a whole jar of very expensive lotion; so much we know, and that is all Mark has to tell us. Matthew adds that it was the disciples who complained; Luke says it was a Pharisee. Perhaps in this instance they were both right, for John's version of the story specifically names Judas as the complainant. That Judas was a Pharisee seems to be the only plausible explanation of what followed.

Who were these Pharisees? They get a 'bad press' in the gospels. Again and again they are attacked for being hypocrites and whited sepulchres and for adhering strictly to the letter of the law and of the prescribed rituals while ignoring the spirit of them. That quite a number of them should be guilty of these things was the inevitable outcome of the sort of movement they belonged to, but it seems that it would be wrong to attribute such qualities to all Pharisees. They were patriots in every sense. They resented the intrusion of Greek culture into Israel. They also resented the decline of Jewish religious practice and of observance of the Jewish law, and accordingly they were themselves very zealous in such practices and observances; this, obviously enough, gave plenty of scope for insincerity and perfunctoriness. Just as in the 1920s the Fascists in Italy, conscious of their country's inglorious showing in the contemporary world, adopted many of the details of ancient Rome in its heyday, so the Pharisees demanded an absolute adherence to what they considered the divinely-inspired dicta of Moses and proclaimed fiercely the glory of Israel in days gone by. (They were aided in this by the researches of the Scribes, which explains why Scribes and Pharisees were sometimes anathematised together). Above all they were nationalists. They longed for both the Roman overlords and the Greek merchants and writers and artists to be driven out of the country. They were not armed rebels; it was not until thirty or forty years later that the militant group, the Zealots, rose in revolt and brought about the destruction by the Romans of Jerusalem. The Pharisees waited patiently for the Messiah. The Messiah would be a descendant of David, and would drive all foreigners from the land and make Israel a strong and unified state in which the Jewish culture would once again flourish, just as David had done a thousand years before.

So Jesus can hardly have been what they expected. There were plenty of peripatetic cranks among the rabbis, and this was all he appeared to them to be. No one could see in him the great leader who would restore Israel – except, apparently, Judas. Judas must have been a man of some vision, who could see in Jesus the possibility of a great nationalist king. Perhaps he saw himself becoming the power behind the throne. At any rate, he threw in his lot with him. But after a time it became clear that here was a man who proclaimed a spiritual kingdom, not a temporal one: who believed in peace, not war: who loved all men, not only the Jews. The gradual realization that his dreams would never be fulfilled must have been terrible indeed to this ardent, ambitious, fervently patriotic, and bitterly disappointed young man. It is not surprising that he felt Jesus had betrayed his people.

The capacity for perpetrating atrocities is not something inherent in either individuals or nations. The full horrors of the Inquisition and its Protestant counterparts, of the genocides carried out the Soviet government in the 1930s, of Belsen and Auschwitz, of Hiroshima, of sadistic personal crimes, are not something that sprang completely conceived and overnight to the minds of especially evil people. Evil is a disease, which, like cancer, grows gradually and attacks ordinary and otherwise healthy people, but which, unlike cancer, can be controlled by the attitude of those whom it attacks; recognized and cast out immediately, it is gone, very likely for ever, but if one attempts to come to terms with it it has already won. Under the stress of tensions and pressures, whether national, political, social, or perhaps just of turpitude, one relaxes a little the code of morals one has always believed to be necessary. Nothing happens, so next time the pressure comes one relaxes a little bit more. And so on. Until in a very short time one's mind has been conditioned to contemplate a deed the very idea of which one would a few months before have dismissed with horror. This progression is inevitable with fanaticism of any kind.

So, we may speculate, it was with Judas. To one of his apparent temperament and interests the betrayal cannot, after months of brooding, have seemed such a terrible deed; in fact it must have appeared a just retribution. Perhaps he saw himself acclaimed a popular hero, going down in history as the far-sighted and resolute figure who had saved his people from the false Messiah.

But he wasn't of course. It was no coup he achieved. It was a petty, spiteful, action. What is more, it was a useless one. As Jesus himself pointed out, he was around and could have been taken anytime. One can hardly imagine anything more futile. The Pharisees were not impressed. Caiaphas, with cynical contempt, paid him for his deed – a payment which he retained sufficient integrity to refuse. He had achieved nothing in the eyes of anybody, but a pain in his own soul from the knowledge that he had betrayed one who had been his friend. There was nothing left for him to do.

Caiaphas

The story of Jesus before the Council in Mark's narrative does not name the High Priest, and neither does that in Luke's, but both Matthew and John name him as Caiaphas. In any case, we know from the historians that Caiaphas succeeded his father-in-law, Annas, sometime between 15 and 18 AD and remained High Priest until 37.

Why Annas had resigned or been deposed we don't know. Perhaps he had fallen foul of one or other of the factions in the Sanhedrin. There were two main parties: the Pharisees, whom we know about, who were the sort of Fascist Party of the time, and the dominant group, the Sadducees. The Sadducees were for maintaining the *status quo* – accepting the Roman domination and the Greek culture, aiming to preserve the Jewish nation by keeping it out of trouble for the time being. And like everyone else who has ever taken a conservative line, in any age and in any matter, they were conservative for a variety of reasons: some because they sincerely believed it to be right, some because it seemed better than any of the conceivable alternatives, some out of sheer laziness or fear of change.

The Jews were autonomous within the Roman Empire. The Roman overlordship did not interfere with Jewish life, so long as Jewish life did not interfere with the Roman overlordship. The centre of Jewish life was the Temple, and because the Jewish religion had been before its decline the very mind and soul and blood of Jewish life, the Temple was cathedral and parliament and law courts all in one. And all three aspects of it were presided over by the High Priest, at this time Caiaphas.

There seems little doubt that Caiaphas was an outstanding figure. It seems that several times Pilate had sought to extend Roman influence and authority in Palestine, to whittle away Jewish autonomy, and each time he had been successfully resisted by Caiaphas, on one occasion even being officially rebuked by the Emperor Tiberius. Caiaphas also had to control his own people. Any sign of rebellion against Rome would have at once brought down the full weight of the Empire on them, the Temple would have been destroyed, and with it the Jewish nation; this actually happened in the year 70, when Caiaphas was dead and the Zealots rose in revolt. But relations with Rome were not the only problem. As a Sadducee Caiaphas had the strongest possible conviction that the Temple must be preserved, as the centre of faith and authority, against all verbal attacks from within Jewry. Therefore a watchful eye had to be kept on all sects and on all unorthodox teachers.

The most unorthodox teacher was Jesus of Nazareth, and he had a large following. He had repeatedly attacked the literal observance of the Law. He had spoken with scorn of the Temple itself. Even so, the Sanhedrin did nothing – until after Palm Sunday. Then something had to be done. A large crowd of people had acclaimed Jesus as King. He began to speak of his 'authority', and on that authority alone he attacked the tradesmen who had set up their stalls in the precincts of the Temple. The authority of the Temple was threatened. By the threat of riots which the Romans would have to put down, the Temple itself was threatened. Large crowds of people in Jerusalem for the Passover were getting over-excited. Disaster was brewing. Action had to be taken, immediate and decisive action; and, thanks to Caiaphas, it was.

An urgent meeting was called to discuss the matter. The story of this is told in John, chapter 11, including Caiaphas' notorious supposed dictum about its being expedient that Jesus should die. A lot hinges on this word 'expedient'. We are used now to political expedience – the sacrifice of principle to the easy way out, the cynical making and breaking of election promises, which we, with equal cynicism, endorse by voting for those who make them. But this, if one studies the text, was by no means what Caiaphas had in mind. The Authorized Version gives us 'It is expedient ...', and so does the Revised Standard Version. The New English Bible, no better, says 'It is to your interest ...' But the Greek word used, συμφερει, normally meant 'It is beneficial'. This is how the Jerusalem Bible tells the story: 'Then the chief priests and the Pharisees called a meeting. "Here is this man working all these signs", they said, "and what action are we taking? If we let him go on in this way everybody will believe in him, and the Romans will come and destroy the Holy Place and our nation". Caiaphas said: "You don't seem to have grasped the situation at all; you fail to see that it is better for one man to die for the people than for the whole nation to be destroyed".'

'It is better for one man to die for the people than for the nation to be destroyed.' Perhaps we might see this as a problem in ethics. But in the first century no one in the world (except possibly Jesus) would have given it a second thought. If a particular life was a threat to law and order, then that life was forfeit; that was unquestionable. Caiaphas, in his capacity as guardian of the temporal and spiritual welfare of the Jewish nation, was bound to take all necessary action to safeguard that welfare. As a Sadducee he couldn't possibly have seen Jesus as anything other than a threat to law and order. As a capable, far-sighted, and energetic administrator, he was bound to remove this threat before it became a reality. We, with the advantage of hindsight, realize that he was mistaken; we know that Jesus was no rabble-rouser but the Prince of Peace. I wonder if we should recognize him as such if he appeared today. But certainly we can't expect his contemporaries to have done so.

To Caiaphas' mind three things must have been necessary to avert the danger to the Temple's authority: to remove the trouble-maker, to discredit him in the eyes of his followers, and to avoid any accusation of causing an innocent man's death in order to play politics. Accordingly, it was necessary that Jesus should die, that he should die ignominiously, and that the Romans should be implicated in his death. How well Caiaphas succeeded in arranging all this we know.

And so the Lamb was slain. It is one of the facts of life that a man's death is in no way governed by his life. Gandhi and Martin Luther King, who throughout their lives passionately rejected violence, were both assassinated; Stalin, the bloodiest man who ever lived, died in his bed.

That Caiaphas was responsible for the death of Jesus is a fact. The whole point is that he was not a malignant, or a callous, or a weak, or a stupid man. He was an upright, able, conscientious, and, we have no reason to doubt, good man. In terms of history, the tragedy of the Crucifixion happened not through any conspiracy of evil, but because this admirable man did his duty.

Pilate

Judas and Caiaphas were Jews, had compelling reasons, bad or good, for wishing Jesus removed, and took active parts in the encompassing of this removal. Pontius Pilate, on the other hand, was not a Jew, had no reason to desire the death of Jesus, and made a passive and negative, though none the less deadly, contribution to the Crucifixion. To the Romans, with their experience of people and nations throughout the known world, this affair of the itinerant teacher whom a few people were hailing, preposterously, as King of the Jews must have seemed trivial indeed – something funny if it was worth noting at all. Certainly there was no possible reason for an execution. But the Jewish authorities clamoured for an execution, and Pilate was involved.

Reading the gospels – all of them – the overwhelming impression one gets is one of weakness, irresoluteness, a desperate attempt to avoid responsibility, on the part of Pilate – who, as he said, could find no fault in Jesus. First he tried to persuade the Jews to judge Jesus themselves; but they pointed out that the crime of which he was accused (presumably causing political unrest) was one that fell within the competence of the Roman authorities. Then, when he heard that Jesus was a Galilean, he tried to get out of it by sending him to Herod Antipas, the ruler of Galilee; but Herod sent him back, since the scene of his alleged crime was Judea. Next, having found him technically guilty but not really deserving of punishment, he hinted that he might be released through the Passover amnesty; but the Jews, prompted doubtless by the Temple authorities, vehemently demanded instead the release of the bandit Barabbas. Then he tried to persuade them that flogging would be a proper and sufficient punishment, but they weren't having that. So he changed his tactics and boldly announced his intention of releasing Jesus; but the crowd was so angry that he withdrew. Finally he let them have their way, but made it clear that the execution would only take place because they wanted it; he publicly washed his hands of responsibility for it.

Why all this shilly-shallying, this wriggling this way and that like a trapped animal? Pilate was a Roman soldier; he can hardly have been squeamish about life and death. He was also a senior executive of the Roman colonial service, so he certainly can't have been afraid of responsibility in general. The only explanation one can think of is that he saw through Caiaphas' plan and was trying desperately to avoid being implicated. Caiaphas obviously wanted Pilate to try Jesus, for two reasons. In the first place Jesus' followers would then, he hoped, blame the Romans rather than the Temple authorities for his death. And in the second place the Roman method of execution was, in Jewish eyes, a much more shameful one. The Jewish method was stoning to death, the Roman one crucifixion, and the cross was seen by the Jews as a symbolic tree. In the book of the Deuteronomy it says that he who dies in a tree is accursed (and you may remember that Absalom died in a tree), so Jesus, it was expected, would be thoroughly discredited by dying this kind of death.

A strong man, of course, would have refused to have anything to do with the matter, and would have been able to bear the consequences. But we know from the historians that Pilate had tried conclusions with Caiaphas before, and Caiaphas had always come off best. What is more, on the one occasion when higher authority had been invoked, Tiberius, Caesar, had sided with Caiaphas. If that should happen again Pilate's job was as good as lost, his career finished. It was safer to take no risks of that kind, even if it did mean a most uncomfortable struggle in his mind.

The thing that hits one about the Passion is, in contrast to the glory of its eternal significance, the ordinariness of the event itself, the ordinariness of the men who brought it about: Judas, the man who allowed his frustration to develop into hate, as any of us might if we didn't watch ourselves; Caiaphas, the man who only did his duty, as any of us would surely hope to do; and Pilate, the man who was afraid of losing his job, as any of us might very well be; the ordinariness of the cross (for centuries artists have shown the cross as towering over the mourners, so that there was something of splendour even in the tragedy: but it seems that in reality the feet of the victim of this common method of executing criminals were a bare two or three inches from the ground); and the ordinariness of our Lord's reaction. He said what any man might say in pain and desolation: 'My God, My God, why have you forsaken me?'

The whole thing is stark, but deeply rooted in the midst of the turbulence, and fluctuations, and commonality, of human life. That is the essence of the Divine Paradox.

THE
HALCYON

The halcyon lay dying.

– At least, one assumed he was dying, for he was incredibly old; no one could remember even when he'd been middle-aged, let alone young. He lay quite still, with his eyes closed, long, thin, with fine but prominent cheekbones. Whether his mind was working one could not have said.

But as a matter of fact it was. A refrain was repeating itself over and over again, a snatch of song from a past before our beginnings, the tune of a slow march.

> Years of our youth and glory.
> Days of our joyful strife.
> We shall be famous in story,
> Though all that we care for is life . . .

That they weren't the right words to the tune he knew, but whether they were words he and his companions had used to sing or private words of his own he no longer had any idea.

Regularly once a second came the thump of the accented notes, matching the placing of the foot on the ground.

Years of our youth and glory.

The parade ground was filled with seemingly countless platoons of men. The parade had marched past, the speeches and ceremonies were over, now came the passing out. 'Move to the left in column of four . . .' A mellow thud from the bass drum and the slow march began.

Days of our joyful strife.

Through the open-ordered ranks of the motionless juniors they went, feet and eyes in pride and unity. Only a few more hours, for at midnight the magic would be on them, studenthood passed.

We shall be famous in story.

Left wheel at the end of the line, quick march in column round the back of the hall, and then, as each platoon neared the front of the parade ground '. . . move into line . . .' This was the wonderful moment, the slow march in line of the leavers, past the saluting base, off the parade ground, and right out of the academy.

All that we care for is life.

Till the last moment the drum persisted, the pervading beat of that special slow march tune reserved for those occasions. – It was a beat that would dominate the lives of some of the marchers for decades to come.

An incomprehensible and discredited enthusiasm. It brought the old creature an easy dying. But how could he have lived with it all those years? Or how could he have lived with the deprivation of it?

THE HARPY

The harpies behaved hatefully, being full of hate. Some of them were saved from hating, and these afterwards affirmed that hate is a very lonely condition.

THE HARRIER

Only a week earlier the whole landscape had been under three feet of snow. But it was the very end of winter. Today the sun shone confidently, and the only patches of white still left were in the most shadowy places. Little clattering streams carried the melted snow excitedly away, and the greenness that emerged was unimaginably bright. It was the sort of afternoon when resurrection seems not a promise but a fact.

The harrier hung motionless above the ridge. Since the air at last was clear he could see a very long way. A dead-straight track ran along the crest of the ridge, dividing it tidily. One side was densely covered with pine and fir trees, not only the ridge itself but the slope and the entire plain beyond, thwarted only by the pale band of a river in the extreme distance. The other side of the track was also thick with conifers on the ridge itself, but towards the bottom of the slope these thinned out and began to give place to other trees and to open spaces – a clearing here, a glade there, and in one place a little meadow.

It was to the plain on this other side that another track, the only branch, led down from the rustic highway along the ridge. Before it reached the plain it passed a solitary building, an inn, set amongst the trees beside a neat garden. At least, one would say it was an inn from the sign hanging out, but one could hardly suppose it to be a commercial venture in that remote spot. Probably it signified that the forester's wife would hospitably furnish a glass of beer and some simple food to whatever infrequent travellers might once in a while pass by.

To the plain beyond there was apparently no limit. The only really prominent physical feature in the whole of it was another ridge, much smaller than the main one, at an angle to it, and some little distance away. It was of irregular shape, with a terrace effect curving up one side of it and ending in a hollow scarp. The trees on this ridge were not evergreens, nor were they huddled together in such profusion as the evergreens, as though to find strength in serried mass. They were in fact beeches; each one of colossal girth, free-standing, self-sufficient, casting no shadow but its own. In the pine woods the light of day was a threat, delicious to contemplate in the security of the half-light; amongst these mighty beeches the light of day was itself security.

There were plenty of lesser features scattered about the plain: knolls, rises, the valleys of brooks. The vegetation also varied; there were copses, heaths, bushy tracts, quite large woods, and open spaces of all kinds and extents. There were as well three man-made features.

The first of these was a village, the shell of a forgotten community, complete with tavern and church, but now in ruins. The roofs and upper walls had gone, and there was no trace of beam or lintel or any wooden part left. This charmingly desolate relic was set in an angle of woodland with open country on the other side and a stream scurrying past the churchyard.

The second was set in the middle of a great flat bare stretch of land, and was a single building, a farmhouse. This was in better repair, for the roof and walls were still complete, but there were no doors or windows.

However, both the farmhouse and the village, notwithstanding their derelict condition, somehow gave the impression that life was unseen rather than absent. The third construction, on the other hand, in spite of being both complete and in excellent repair, appeared indubitably dead. But this was to some extent an illusion, for just as the trees which stand like skeletons all through the winter have innumerable buds lying dormant within them, so this tower in spite of its deadness seemed to hold more promise than the other buildings. Perhaps it was simply hope.

It was hard to say for what end the tower might have been intended. Some towers are built from mere caprice, or to fix a focus into the landscape, in which case there is a touch of whimsy about them, an air of folly which more than justifies the name. Some towers are built to demonstrate a new material, or a new technique of construction, and with these the character of the inventor quite evidently overrides that of the architect for as long as the tower stands. But this tower was so very right. It obtruded without being obtrusive. It was tall without either stretching or embarrassment. It was spare without being slender. It was purposeful without giving any hint of what its purpose was or had been. It was strong and silent but not truculent. It had not a brick or a finial unnecessary to its function, yet was by no means stark and unlovely. It was alone but not, apparently, abandoned. It was self-confident without being brash, invulnerable without being haughty, proud yet not without humility. It was a sum-of-all-things sort of tower.

It must be understood that these various features of the landscape were at several miles' distance from the ridge and from one another. The tower was in the very centre of the plain.

The sun was already sinking, turning the ribbon of water beyond the forest from pearly silver to a fierce vermilion, when a horseman emerged from the wood opposite the forester's house and rode slowly up the track on to the ridge. As he reined his horse to turn where the tracks joined he lifted his head and displayed a face gripped, one would say, by powerfully moving thoughts, melancholy though far from despairing. He stopped directly underneath the harrier, let go the reins, and remained sitting there, a stiffly upright figure but with head bent forward till his chin rested on his breast.

So much was there for all to see. What followed was some kind of spectral image, phantom sights and sounds reflected as it were from the mind of the horseman to that of the harrier.

As dusk fell lights began to flicker on one by one in the village (at that time apparently neither ruined nor deserted). Horses could be heard approaching, and soon a troop of hussars clattered cheerfully into the square. They formed into line and awaited the order to dismount. The officer surveyed them with pride and pleasure before giving the command, and then with much playful rudery they went off to see to their horses. Afterwards they made a big fire in the middle of the square, squatting round it to eat their rations.

Meanwhile the villagers had nearly all come out of doors. They mingled with the soldiers, laughing and chatting gaily, giving them ham and sausage and fresh rye bread. The soldiers in return dug deep into their knapsacks to produce little simple toys for the children, and pressed the grown-up girls to drink from their flasks. The officer stood watching affectionately. Presently he spied another young woman, of refined appearance, who had not come outside but was leaning on an upstairs windowsill of the inn regarding the scene with quiet enjoyment. He went over and stood by the wall of the inn, his head thrust back, talking earnestly up at her. From time to time she replied, nodding and smiling gently.

After a while they fell silent. Then he recollected that they must be off about their business, and shouted an order to the soldiers. These got to their feet, stepped out the fire, and prepared to remount. The officer's horse was brought and he sprang on to the saddle, where standing upright he could just reach to kiss the girl in the window. By this time the soldiers were mounted and in line; on the command they turned into column and walked off into the darkness. The villagers shouted their good-byes, then went back into their houses. One after another the lights went out.

Meanwhile something was just beginning to happen over at the farm. One or two rifle shots cracked out, leading to more steady firing. The snicker of a bren gun joined in, and an arc of red hyphens told that tracer was being used. Then a flare was sent up; though they stopped dead immediately, a curved line of men advancing on the farm was revealed. As the light of the flare died away every firearm in the vicinity broke out demoniacally.

The young officer in the farmhouse felt the blood leap like a mountain torrent in his veins. He and his men had occupied the abandoned farm in the morning, and all day they had striven to dig trenches in the hard earth. They had finished only shortly before dark, and since then had still and silently awaited the attack they knew must come. It was the young officer's first engagement. He felt a tremendous exhilaration, similar to but infinitely greater than that he had felt in some important rugby football match at school. The sight of the enemy (only he thought of them not as the enemy but as opponents) kneeling motionless in the sudden light became one of the most enduring pictures in his memory.

Another flare went up. This time there was not an attacker to be seen; the farm must have been better defended than they had expected. But perhaps another attack would come in the sleepy hours of morning. For the moment at any rate the firing died away, and all was silent in that area.

One became aware of singing in the forest along the ridge – soldiers' songs, filled as such songs are with a mixture of bravado and homesickness. There are several sadnesses in war; a tragic sadness for many, a sordid sadness for many more, and for just a few a romantic and inspiring sadness. These songs seemed to foreshadow something of all three. All along the ridge, just off the track on both sides, one noticed fires in the forest, and round these the soldiers were gathered, holding their hands to the blaze as they sang.

Some kind of vehicle was approaching from the end of the ridge. It was a large old-fashioned motor car, with the grand-ducal arms on the door. Inside, wearing field uniform, was the new young reigning prince (his father's body scarcely cold in the vault, himself without hair on his lip). His fairy-like and even younger consort was beside him. They were a high-minded couple, determined anxiously to guide their principality into happiness; and then the war had been suddenly thrust upon them before they had had a chance to start.

The car stopped. The driver (alone in front, for the ADC had gone before) sat like stone. The young couple conversed urgently, trying to keep back the dread that was creeping round their hearts. It was mostly the Grand Duchess who spoke, the glowing end of her cigarette bobbing up and down frantically as she did so.

At length they both knew the time had come. The Grand Duke got out, saluted, and watched the car drive off. Then he strode into the forest towards one of the fires.

Gradually the singing died away; the fires burned down to a glimmer and disappeared. The lone horseman on the ridge stretched himself, swept his eyes round the sky, and rode off down the hill.

All was one pitch black mass now; nothing of the landscape could be distinguished at all. Except the tower. Round this (or perhaps beyond it, but at any rate not emanating from it) was a faint glow, just sufficient to show that it was still there, dependable if unfathomable. And in the window of the little inn or forester's house there were lights.

THE HERMIT

Different species of humming birds were to be found in different parts of the jungle. There was one particular profusely-flowered hollow, three or four hundred metres from the river and a couple of kilometres from the village, which a solitary hermit took as his. I watched him often, for hours at a time. He was a happy soul. Though always on his own he never seemed to be alone. It was as though he had some companion whom I couldn't see.

THE HERON

The heron woke up feeling somehow as though it were her last day as a fully-fledged person. Today she was going to enter – well it wasn't really an institution, but it felt as though it were. The idea of going to this place made her feel unwanted. Which annoyed her, because she knew she wasn't unwanted; she didn't have to go, she just felt it would be better. She was very old, too old to be certain of being able to fend for herself much longer. Where she was going, she felt, was the right sort of place for someone like her.

There used to be at that time an area where the hills were naked, a noman's land, a place completely without vegetation. Except for one, large, dead, tree. On the branches of this tree sat herons, white ones, countless numbers of them. If one had seen a picture of them one would have said the artist was a poor one for he had painted a picture without life, so still and noiseless were they.

Our heron saw it with dismay. But she was a stout-hearted bird, and not disposed to turn back. Her eye fell on a vacant branch, and she proceeded to perch there. Not one of the other birds made the slightest sound or movement. It evidently made no difference to them whether she was there or not.

But in time, in many weeks, the resources within her had made themselves apparent to them all. The other birds came to be grateful for her presence among them, and so did she.

THE
IORA

The iora regarded his imminent commencement at the university with considerable trepidation. There had been a lot of student violence recently – not really over any specific issue, just general intransigence. There had been persecution by vociferous factions of individual students whom they looked on as dissidents. There had been drowning-out of visiting speakers, sometimes accompanied by physical assault. And there had been apparently senseless damage done repeatedly to the fabric and installations of the university itself. All this had been going on to such an extent that the routine cliché-ridden protests had passed unnoticed. The prevailing climate was bigotry.

Once arrived and in residence the iora remained for many days overwhelmed by the scale of the place. One scurried about, from room to lecture hall to restaurant, apparently without identity, like some anonymous ant in an enormous colony. However, in time one got used to that.

But as he settled down and became capable of observing his surroundings, what worried him was how little the students bothered to communicate with one another. They got together in little cliques and endlessly developed their pet phobias, and that

66

was all. His impression of the university was of a vast wasteland dotted not with oases but with little pockets of ignorance and intolerance.

THE JUNCO

Towards the end I visited the junco often, though it needed a superlative effort to stomach the squalidity of his room. There was utter degradation in every aspect of his being. I asked him once what the point of it all was, and this is what he told me.

'Well, you see, it was instant unloneliness. You could fill your life with whatever companions you could desire, and it was all so easy. Life became gay and untroubled and full of promise. And your friends were there, and were whom you wanted, and they did what you wanted. After a while they began to fade, but you could summon them back again, any time.

'But the trouble was that eventually things became more shadowy, no better than imaginings, and then you had to do it more often and in stronger doses. In the end it becomes a mad rush to clutch at things before they fade. And there's always the dread that they will be gone for ever if you can't produce the wherewithal for the stuff. And so ordinary interests must be put aside, and you must hang on with all you've got to this one idea of always being able to renew the magic.'

THE KAKODORI

Restlessness is in my blood. Ever since I was born I've moved from place to place every few months, at first on my father's account and then on my own. In all that time I have only once left anywhere reluctantly. It happened very many years ago, when I was young (though fully grown) and for the first time was meeting others as an individual and not as an appendage of my parents.

I knew from the first day that here was somewhere I wanted to stay, and I also knew I had no control over how long I should stay and that it couldn't be for more than two or three months. Well, after a time the blow fell and I heard that I must go in a matter of weeks, leaving all those whom my newly-discovered capacity for relationships had made dear.

In a panic I fluttered to the hills. It was autumn and the round valleys were dense with the deep red maples – like bowls of *rødgrød* said a friend who aspired to satire. I fled to the shore, and discovered a fellow feeling where sad and twisted pines ride out the salted winds. The rocks were bound together with ropes of straw; no such bonds, alas, held us. I visited vast bronzes in the cool of ancient halls; but neither the *yogan-in* nor the *semui-in* were for me.

By a certain plain I thought of Basho's epigram on a battlefield. He told of the breeze, of the grass, of long-forgotten graves, of those who fell, of their high hopes, of the glory of the dead and the limbo of those who lived a little longer, of the pain of those who waited in vain and the joy (lasting or otherwise) of those who waited not in vain, of how the war is still remembered but the cause of it is ages since forgotten, of the uselessness of it all, of the transience of men's desires, of soldiers and of battles and of wars throughout eternity, of life itself, and again of the wind ruffling the tops of the singing grass where long ago men singing fought and their bones are perhaps still to be found in the soil beneath the grass. – How could he say all that in seventeen syllables?

And then the time was quite upon us. In misery we waved as I was drawn away. And, as it chanced, the popular song of the moment was also a lamentation of farewell. Trite doubtless it was, but since it fitted our mood it seemed real enough. Blared from loudspeakers at every station on the way, for twenty-four hours it bored into me, so that I can still recall every note and word.

At length, on the distant coast, another three days I waited, dark beginning-of-winter days. The shore was desolate. The islands in the bay seemed to be awaiting some imminent signal when they would sink from view. Now after all these years I struggle to remember how it could have been that I left without being physically abducted.

THE KILLDEER

There was a childless couple who very much wanted to be parents. After a while an unwanted fertilized egg turned up and was given to them. They hatched it and reared the young bird with tender care, and they and the young bird became a family. But eventually the bird who had laid the egg claimed the young bird and, as was her right, had to have him. The bereavement of the parents was almost unbearable. The shock to the young bird was profound and damaging. Why did the egg-layer do that? Was it loneliness? Or was it possessiveness? Or is there in fact any difference between those two things?

THE KINGFISHER

Before there was you and I,
Before there was you,
There was I.
And I was wide and under the sun
And early and late on the streams
Of the sky-long summit of hours,
And high through the brilliant heart of day
I shone in the breath of time.

And then there was you
And the dayspring bowed
And the weather fled over the hill
And the call of the trumpets died in their throats
As the wind no longer blew.
And now I am rueless although
Before there was you and I
There was I
Before there was you.

THE
KING OF SAXONY

He was of course meant to be conspicuous, but he seemed so very vulnerable as he sat there by himself, physically tiny and dwarfed, almost crushed, by the immense plumes in his headdress. A private life was scarcely allowed him; everything had to be done in the full view of a critical public; relaxation was rare and escape out of the question. His good actions would remain unnoticed, his bad would bring instant execration. Advice he could take, if he could find anyone to give it, but if he was badly advised the blame would still fall on him alone. And such was the eminence of the station he found himself in, its uniqueness, that there was none qualified to proffer advice on many matters; consequently his very apartness was potentially an occasion of disaster.

But nature adjusts itself wonderfully well. No doubt a situation that calls for especial toughness itself develops that toughness. Surrounded by enemies, he nevertheless survived and enabled his flock to survive. He fulfilled his function to perfection, in a way that other species signally failed to do.

THE
KISKADEE

The sugar plantation had been given up to a housing estate, and it was a long time since anyone had seen a cane punt on the trench. From a distance the water seemed to be shining white in the early morning sunlight, and the bushes overhanging its banks softened and sinuated its outlines and shut out the neighbourhood till it seemed really a tropical idyll. This was an illusion. The trench was full of slime and all kinds of filth, and the water was too thick to see through, even to the depth of half an inch. Water hyacinth was growing along both banks and beginning to spread towards the middle; at least it hid the floating corpses of dogs and kids.

On the downhanging dead lower frond of a sago palm leaning over the trench a kiskadee was sitting, looking this way and that, uttering his familiar greeting, backchatting all who passed by. He was a comedian, this one. Speak to him and he would put his head on one side and lift a wing as though to shrug his shoulders. Then he would cackle, jump, turn round in the air, and land again to bow and joke with the next comer. Every morning, when it wasn't raining, he would do this, as though to convince the world and himself of business as usual.

When he returned to the nest the sadness caught him again. It was always like that since his loved one's departure. (The kiskadee had been jilted.) It annoyed him that he couldn't escape this melancholy, because it seemed to him it was self-pity. And he was not even sure that he had wanted to mate anyway, or with that particular female. Yet the sense of loss was there and would not be shaken off. After a very short time he could no longer bear the nest, and flew off to the top of a star-apple tree to meditate.

His was a shallow personality, thought the kiskadee. When he and his lady had met there had been no deep-seated attraction, no careful weighing of the conveniences and inconveniences, merely a mutual assumption that they would mate. But this mating, he had felt, was something he wanted to have done rather than to do, and once or twice he had thought of breaking out of it before it was too late, but his essential good nature prevented him from perhaps hurting the other. However, it hadn't taken him long to become accustomed to the idea of mating, and then to be enthusiastic about it.

A strident courtship it had been. They were always to be seen, chasing from tree to tree, laughing and quarrelling, the centre of a crowd of equally gaudy companions. Life may have been trivial, but it was very amusing. Then had come the time to settle down. The kiskadee loved it, and came more and more to care for his mate, who was the centre of it. She too loved it, or so it had seemed. Life became fuller for them both.

But something went wrong, impossible to say what. Day by day she grew less contented, felt something was missing, became in turns irritable and listless. Finally one morning she left the nest and didn't come back. He never did discover exactly what the trouble was, and quite possibly she never really knew.

Why does everything seem so empty? thought the kiskadee. He was young and able and energetic; there was plenty he could do, any number of places to go, and nothing now to hold him back. There were plenty of other birds to choose a lady friend from, and he'd never had much in common with that one. And yet life had a hole in it, a desperate, aching, hole, which felt quite unfillable. But it's only a matter of time, he told himself; in a few weeks I shall have forgotten. Time. He stamped his foot on the branch. Time; he must hold on to that.

Suddenly he soared into the sky and flew away very fast. Really I'm extremely lucky to be so free, he told himself, rather in the way an unhungry man politely accepts a piece of rich cake he doesn't want. His determination couldn't melt the lead in his heart, but it did a good job of disguising it. He swooped down to the path and began to show off as of old, full of cheek and raillery, an audacious remark for every passer-by. Only the discerning could see the slight signs of tightening around his lower eyelids.

THE KIWI

The kiwi has a remarkable gift of divination; bury food some distance below the surface of the ground, and he will find it without delay. Actually this is because he has extremely sensitive nostrils at the tip of his rod-like beak. But to some it appears a supernatural gift; and there are those who, perhaps from fear or perhaps from jealousy, feel called upon to shun if not to manhandle anyone singled out for such a gift. This is perhaps why the kiwi is a solitary and rather pugnacious bird, and why he has developed such a leathery thick skin.

THE KOOKABURRA

The kookaburra was always laughing. Some thought it a disease. Some thought he was either foolish or insane. Some thought it improper not to take things seriously. But the kookaburra didn't care. He felt his laughter was not only moral but positively healing. Those who had most to do with him often found it had a therapeutic effect on them too. But others, perhaps enviously, decided good-humour was a sin.

THE
LAPWING

The lapwing wasn't sure why or by whom he'd been invited. He looked round the field nervously. There were numbers of seagulls, of starlings, of pheasants, of blackbirds, of crows, and one or two jackdaws. But there was no other lapwing, and no one he knew at all.

They were all enjoying themselves hugely, making considerable uproar by mere conversation. They all talked at once, and much more loudly than was necessary. They laughed in an over-hearty way at a succession of far from funny jokes. They expressed exaggerated delight at meeting one another whom they usually tried to avoid. They showed off in a way they wouldn't have tolerated from their children.

The lapwing wandered about pretending to attach himself now to this group now to that. He nibbled nervously at any supposed delicacy to show he was occupied, then too soon found himself empty-handed and had to reach for another in order not to appear at a loose end. Occasionally someone unusually observant would noice his predicament and kindly say something to him. But he found himself quite frozen by his embarrassment, and in any case he was never very good at making natural replies to unnatural remarks.

The feeling of exclusion brought about by being among such a crowd of birds who all knew one another but didn't know him was overwhelming. His sense of duty demanded that for the sake of appearances he should stick it bravely for a little while. But as soon as he decently could, he fled.

THE LARK

It was that glad sort of day of which the overwhelming impression is blueness, not the burning blue of less temperate climates, but a softer though equally sunny blue.

If one had been lying on one's back in the meadow (as well one might have on such a day), one would have seen a lark fly straight up, rapturously, as though trying to touch the blue. And then suddenly she turned lazily over, swooped downwards again, looped, and once more rose. This and similar performances were repeated for many minutes.

It was a gratuitous display of joy, the self-abandon of one who has suddenly perceived the face of God on a summer's day and rejoices in being alone and at one with him.

THE LEGHORN

The morning began with the crowing of a cock. This always seemed symbolic of the difference between country life and city life.

As the sun began to show up the features of the valley he went outside and looked round his property. It was a broad flat valley with a stream running through it and low but protective hills curving on either side as though in a fond embrace. There were meadows and copses, and a small mill turned by the stream. A proportion of the valley was cultivated; he grew and made sufficient to satisfy his own needs entirely. There was no other habitation for miles around, and he seldom saw anyone. He was perfectly content like that. As he gazed about the valley he thought how perfect his existence was: a day of physical labour, idyllic surroundings, an evening of leisure to enjoy as he would, a peaceful night – no worries, nothing owed to anyone; what more could he want?

A drop of rain fell, and he turned indoors again. It had not always been like this. Once he had lived in a big city and had had many friends. But it seemed there was always something on one's mind; if one could enjoy life at all it was by feverishly throwing oneself at it. In spite of all his friends there were times when he was alone, odd afternoons when he had no arrangements. How lonely he was on those occasions. Sometimes he would turn up to invitations hours early in an effort to escape that loneliness. Or he would walk in the city, staring at people; everyone would seem to have a companion or be one of a party except himself. He stared into shops, into cafés, into buses, everywhere people were talking, heedless of him who alone of those millions had no one to talk to.

It was a heavy but short shower. The time after rain was his favourite. He loved the faster running of the stream, the dripping of the leaves, the fresh smell of everything, the general feeling of purification. He thought again how lucky he was (and also how strange it was that he needed no companion now: how he'd only felt the need of one so long as he was among others who had one).

Times of day, times of year, always turned up in due course, always at the right time, always when they were needed. The earth pushed up an abundance and variety of things which were in perfect complement to one another and all that a reasonable being could ask for. He was complete.

But his cousin the buff leghorn was a bird of a very different colour, though equally happy.

The buff leghorn stretched and turned over, and thought how good it was to be in town. Born and brought up in the country, he had always felt somewhat out of things in the close-knit and unadventurous community which for twenty years was all he had known of the world. Here in the city one met every kind and could choose one's friends. He had quickly developed satisfying relationships.

THE
LINNET

When the west wind sets the slender lilies gently swaying,
People such as you are often out and idly straying.
Where you go there is no sorrow, and the path is broad and
    smooth,
So your footsteps in the garden seem always to be saying.
And to their beat so light and charming, to the rhythm of their
    pace,
Like a songlet in my head these words are always playing.

(After a ghazal of Keller's)

THE
LOON

The loon was mad. It was a fairly cheery sort of madness, for he
suffered none of the black rage or depression that others so afflicted
sometimes do. On the contrary, he was able to people his world
with whomever he pleased.

   But there had been a time when he had inhabited the weird half-
world between madness and sanity. That had been a time of
suspicion and of dread. And, too, it had been a lonely time, for he
had had neither the company of the sane nor the refuge of the
deluded.

THE LOVEBIRD

No longer young,
Her songs all long since sung,
She wanders, petulant, about the town,
The corners of her mouth turned down.

THE LYREBIRD

Atop a swansdowned alabaster bed
And plucking listlessly at this and that
Was Ariadne.
Always she sat on the icy couch
And dreamed of Attic forests
And wandering naked hand in hand
While Attic shepherds played an intermezzo.
But walking in the Naxian woods
In the bark of every tree
And in the lichen on every rock
The pale sardonic face of Theseus lurked.

THE MACAW

He was a large blue and yellow bird, in a cage not all that much bigger than himself. He sat still; there was nothing else he could do. He thought of the panther in Rilke's poem, whose eyes had become so tired with staring through the bars that they no longer saw anything; it seemed to the panther that the bars stood a thousand deep, and beyond them was nothing. The macaw understood this so well. What was the good of anything? Hope was the only salvation. His hope had been taken away. To remove one's capacity for hope is surely, he thought, the cruellest of all crimes.

THE MAGPIE

Many years after the catastrophe I visited the ruin. Nature had claimed it, and it was a hard struggle to force a way through the undergrowth and reach the house. The walls were still standing, but behind them was a hostile mass of vegetation. Everywhere on the terraces, on the steps, between the feet of the statues, young sycamores had thrust themselves. But the ghosts were there, the friendly ghosts of what had been. It was pleasant if melancholy to sit on the balustrade an hour or two in the decadent peace which had succeeded the active peace of former days.

Years later again I went there once more. With the changing circumstances of life the place had ceased to be remote. It had become a jollying spot for the people of the town. They had trodden down the undergrowth, so the house could once again be seen. But they had surrounded it with the litter of their being, the cans and cartons of their sustenance, the magnified throbbing chords of their existence. The ghosts had gone, and no sort of peace remained. The loneliness of it all was too much for me.

THE MARTIN

Slowly
Like the Dutchman's songs
That floated on the wind
The turning leaves went drifting
From the park beneath the trees
Along the rusty alleys
To the river,
And like threads of memory
From a window in the gaunt grey house
The violin notes hung:

Along the fading avenues of days we heard
The solitary soft singing of September
Upon the ardent air.

THE MERLIN

Of all that the Toompea has seen and suffered through the centuries its chestnuts and lindens seem to express a lot. These are stubborn and enduring trees, yet by no means without grace. Their stance, however, is a little defensive, a little withdrawn; the undiscerning might even call it sullen. But they are unquestionably *there*, and so appropriately there. The squares would be bare indeed without them, yet somehow one is surprised that they are not bare.

One damp June day on one of the lindens not far from the archway through to the Lükike Jalg, a merlin sat and brooded. How long must this silent endurance of the foreign occupation go on? The worst thing about it was the feeling that no one outside cared. If only they could be assured that there was some sympathy and concern for them overseas things wouldn't seem so hopeless, he felt. As it was, isolated and forgotten, and now all but submerged, what would become of them?

THE
MINIVET

In the city of the minivets no one behaves openly. They all peer at one another from behind curtains. As you walk down the street you are conscious of being watched; like lightning you turn your eyes, but all you see is the faint swish of a curtain back into place. All day, every day, they stand at the parlour window, beak and beady eye restlessly moving up and down the crack looking for something.

Perhaps if they went out and met one another they wouldn't have to wonder.

THE
MISTLETOE BIRD

When the mistletoe bird was out with some new found acquaintances and it came to his round he really had to screw himself up to take the necessary action, and frequently didn't manage it. He just couldn't get over the fear of pushing himself forward, of appearing to show off.

'Freeloading' is a practice obviously and rightly frowned on. Yet perhaps (except in the case of those who make a living by it) apparent freeloading is more often the result of shyness than of meanness.

THE
MOCKINGBIRD

'Liebknecht could not stand this.
He did not mind in the least being called
a traitor to his country, but he could
not tolerate being laughed at.'
  The Kings Depart, Richard M. Watt.

It isn't really strange that the most brutally spoken debaters, who can take equally brutal speaking in return, find themselves demoralized by mockery. There is a terrible feeling of isolation in mockery. So long as we are responded to seriously, however opposedly, we know that we are recognized; but mockery implies that we are of no account.

THE
MONAL

At swantide of an eager year
The waters of the lake rose in an afternoon
And spilled into the grotto over the very windowsill
Where the young princess had used to sit and smoke.

She fled then to the ferny hillsides
Where hares remained and pheasants hung against a blueblack
  sky
And the far-off clamour of the Rostovs' wolf hunt
Was heard above the breeze.

She watched, heard, half attending,
Old plays and concerts no one else remembered,
Pursued half-smilingly the willing dragonfly
('Libélula vaga de una vaga ilusión')
And waited for some brave hussar in cardiganned pelisse
Fresh from the winter war in Poland
Or, like the Sonatina princess, for a China prince.

For the windbell sings
Of a land beyond the river's edge,
A land of jade and silk and rubies
And quite inexorable smiles.

THE MOORHEN

A great scarlet waterfowl flapping through space
With a nonchalant grin on the front of her face.

A fish who needs coffee in which to survive
Because water's too washy to keep her alive.

A cat who can chatter with real human words,
Who eats with a spoon, and who never kills birds.

Alas, but not one of these creatures exists,
For eccentrics burn off like the midsummer mists.

A brave new society just cannot do
With those who've a bold individual view.

THE
MUTTONBIRD

The muttonbird may have been muddle-headed but he sometimes managed to bang the odd nail more or less on the head. Once he said:

'It is our endeavour to love one another. This is what we are commanded to do, and if we are not trying to fulfil that command then we have no justification for claiming to be disciples of Jesus Christ. But many of us find, I suspect, that there are those whom it is easier to love at a distance. Well, if that happens we can get away from them, for some of the time if not for all. But there are those who can't get away. All day and every day they are cooped up with the same companions, regardless of compatibility. In those circumstances I'm inclined to think that love may become a somewhat more difficult exercise.'

THE
MYNAH

There is a particular garden not far from the sea in a hot and damp land. This garden consists mainly of a large oblong of coarse grass, surrounded by hibiscus hedge. Down one side there is a row of coconut palms, and in the middle stands a very matriarch among mango trees. There are other trees, and shrubs, and various bright green articles which doubtless aspire to be trees, and flowers, and plants which have resigned themselves to a spinsterhood of flowerlessness, and a neat L-shaped planting of balabalas smothered in magenta orchids.

In one corner of the garden is a house. It is a substantial house, built partly of stone and partly of wood, loftily thrusting a broad flagged verandah towards the garden as though in a gesture of irritated *de facto* inferiority despite a *de jure* superiority. – There is no denying that the house seems to be a feature of the garden, rather than the garden an adjunct to the house.

A soft breeze blows perpetually from over the sea, seldom so much as rustling the leaves, but keeping the garden cool. Most of the time it brings rain. In dry weather the grass is soft and oozy; in wet weather it becomes a swamp. The only apparent vegetable activity is the occasional sudden fall of a frond or a coconut with a muddy thud to the ground. Toads stalk about, and lizards, little shiny brown ones, show themselves when the sun is shining. A large rat often makes his way along the ditch beyond the hibiscus.

But it is to the birds that the garden really seems to belong. Bulbuls, fruit doves, shrike-bills, sun birds, honeyeaters of various types, parrot finches, all come regularly; and of course the mynahs. The mynahs, some of them, nest in the eaves of the house, using all sorts of garish rubbish to make a slipshod home, its whereabouts indicated by streamers of recording tape. These mynahs, both resident and visiting, will sit coarsely shouting on the railing of the verandah, heedlessly soiling as they converse, from time to time strutting to the open door and staring aggressively in.

In the house live (amongst other creatures) two cats. These consider the garden their domain too, and sometimes in sunny weather they will venture outside to endeavour an assertion of their right. Their attitudes to the birds differ. Both see them as unpleasant beings, foreign alike in nature and in habit, but while the first cat thinks these attributes disqualify them from taking part in society and wishes to banish them from the neighbourhood of decent folk, the second believes they have every right to be odd and nasty provided they don't seek to impose themselves on others.

If only a few mynah birds are about when a cat emerges from the house they will at once fly away. But they soon return, bringing a gang of friends. Then they perch on the branches of whichever tree the cat is nearest to and set up a loud continual hoarse rude chatter. If the cat moves they move, all the time edging closer to her, shouting yet more loudly and angrily, pointedly displaying the sharpness of their bills, daring the cat to make a move towards one of them, when the rest would immediately descend on her and tear her to pieces. The menace is so sure that in a very short time the cat will have retreated into the house.

This attitude of the mynahs is not born in fear; rather they have a derisive confidence in the strength of their numbers. It seems that cats stand for something they have decided to hate. And when hate arises, reason and tolerance and civilized behaviour must vanish.

THE NIGHTINGALE

It was dusk in the forest. The tree-frogs and cicadas were tuning up, and the fireflies moved about like dainty usherettes. The nightingale was about to begin her performance, apparently with the confidence of an established star. As she waited she mused on her success.

She had the finest voice ever heard; everyone was agreed. The range, the power, the purity, the artistry, were beyond compare. Glissandos, faultless and of astonishing rapidity; coloratura, of a richness and variety unsurpassed; a haunting melodic presentation; a bubbling vitality; – all these were hers. An orchid of mystery, a rose of complexity, a daisy of honesty and simplicity, her voice could be any of these. The greatest people of the day had travelled hundreds of miles to hear her, and kept her singing encores till the dawn.

But all that was long ago.

Tonight as soon as she opened her mouth one knew that here was no singer. Her voice was harsh and cracked and listless. She kept losing the key. The top notes she couldn't begin to reach; the low notes were merely a croak. There was hardly anyone there to hear her, but those who were gave her a scattering of applause, half polite and half ironic.

Tonight at last she recognized what everyone else had known for years. She was a has-been.

THE NIGHTJAR

The nightjar turned out the light and got into bed. She lay awake for a time, enjoying the peace and restfulness of just lying on her back entirely relaxed in the dark.

She was just drifting off to sleep when she became aware of voices. They sounded directly below her. She woke fully again and strained to listen. They were not unfriendly voices, merely conversational. As far as she could judge there were only two of them, and she couldn't make out a word they were saying. She listened, frightened, for a while, and then got up and very cautiously went round the house. The voices were not *in* the house: that she soon established. She peered from behind the curtains of each window, but could see nothing. The odd thing was that as she moved about the house the sound of the voices got neither louder nor softer. She went back to her own room and stood irresolutely beside the bed. The voices stopped, but it was a long time before she got back into bed.

It was even longer, once in, that she lay there, for she was too disturbed for sleep to come. Then, when the background noises of late evening had given place to the real silence of night, a slow sawing sound began. Again she lay and listened, more frightened than before. The sound appeared to be coming from just outside the window of her room. Slowly she slid out of bed and tiptoed fearfully to the curtain. She contrived to see behind it without moving it. There was nothing there, and the sound now seemed to originate further along the house. It was a steady sound, without the pause at the end of each piece of wood that would normally be part of a sawing operation. She moved stealthily round the house in pursuit of it, but wherever she was the sound was somewhere else. It stopped as suddenly as it had started.

She had just got back into bed when the voices started again. At least she thought they were starting again, but she soon found they were different voices. There were many of them this time, gay but somehow unearthly. They grew louder as they approached, seemed to circle the house two or three times, then died away again.

The next disturbance was a tapping, which started about quarter of an hour later. A light tapping it was, an inquisitive rather than a demanding tapping. Once again she stalked it all over the house, and once again failed to locate it. It stopped, as the other noises had, which brought the nightjar a temporary feeling of relief, even though she couldn't believe that something else wouldn't start soon. In fact the tapping started again, within a very few minutes, this time at a different tempo. It went on for a long time, with varying pauses, and in varying patterns. Sometimes it was fast, sometimes in little runs, sometimes in rhythmic groups, but always gentle. Just as she thought she couldn't stand it and was about to run from the house, it stopped again, this time for good.

Almost immediately she heard laughter – not a menacing laughter, just quiet chuckles. It appeared to come from the front door. She went to the back door. It was there too. No escape. Fortunately it didn't last long; but she could no longer contemplate going through either door.

For a long time after that there was no sound at all. After the first few minutes she began to find the utter (unnatural it seemed) silence even more unnerving than the noises. But in time her nerves slackened and she went back to bed.

The series of fears had taken up several hours, and she was exhausted. Sleep began to overtake her in spite of her jitteriness. How long she'd dozed she couldn't say, but again she suddenly found herself wide awake listening to a new sound. This was a kind of soft scraping. It might have been somebody slowly rubbing his shoes on one of those brush affairs which used to be set beside the backdoors of well-to-do houses. It might have been a dog scratching his back on the branch of a bush. It might have been someone carefully removing the putty round a window-pane. It might have been a hundred things. It went on and on and on and on, the pace never varying by the millionth of a second, constant, insistent, defeating any possible attempt to ignore it or shut it out. This time she didn't get out of bed, but simply lay in terror and awaited what would happen.

Before it had finished more voices began. These were quiet but menacing. There were three or four of them; at first they spoke in turn, then at the same time but against one another, then in unison like some kind of chant. This became a sort of chilling whisper that left no doubt of evil intent. However, it didn't last long, and when it stopped the nightjar was conscious that the scraping had stopped too.

Again there was a long period of silence. The nightjar had no thought of sleep now, but she did hope that the silence would last till dawn. But just as she began to relax there was a sudden loud knocking – not a steady knocking but an obvious demand for entrance. She sprang out of bed and rushed to the sound. – At least a real live thing, however brutal, would be better than the disembodied sounds; here was a companion, even if he coshed her. But when she reached the sound it had moved elsewhere. At the same time it was accompanied by callous laughter. Whichever way she turned it was behind her. She put her hands to her head and screamed.

She must at last have stopped screaming, because she became aware of a police-car siren. It was approaching rapidly. The relief afforded by this sound was indescribable. The agony was over. In just a few seconds now the car would arrive and friendly men would be there to protect her. The sound slowed and revived as the car came round the corner fifty yards away. Now it was right outside the house. She listened for it to stop, for the sound of a handbrake being applied and that of doors slamming. All she heard was the wail of the siren disappearing into the distance.

The disappointment was intense. All hope was gone now. The laughter restarted, mocking and sadistic. Footsteps approached. She was gripped by the utmost terror. The laughter sounded in her ears, and she fainted.

When she awoke she was lying on the floor of the sitting-room, which was filled with sunshine. She got up and went round the house. All the doors and windows were securely locked, and there was no sign of any disturbance. She sat down and thought. Someone or something had been trying to demoralize her. The thought that intrigued her was how much less demoralized she would have been if she had had someone else, anyone, in the house with her.

THE NUTHATCH

On Sunday afternoons in passive cities
Walking the streets alone and in the rain
One finds a zenith of ecstatic loneliness
And memories not of one's childhood
But of long before,
Of coloured lithographs and German toys,
Of trams and factory chimneys in
Yorkshire or Prussian Saxony,
Grey compositions of a silent ache
For an almost remembered
Someone else's youth.

What can it mean –
This longing for a time I never knew?

THE
OSTRICH

'I have become the jackal's brother and the ostrich's companion'.
    (Job, ch.30, v.29)

Suffering is a tremendous problem for us all, and for many people the existence of suffering is an insurmountable barrier to faith. How, they say, can we believe in God (especially in a loving God) when there is so much suffering in the world?

Much suffering can be blamed on the sinfulness of man, notably war and poverty, and all the physical and mental anguish caused by cruelty and violence and bitterness, and by just plain failure to care. But this doesn't explain pain and disease, bereavement, and natural disasters like floods and hurricanes and earthquakes.

There is a school of thought (which seems to draw its inspiration not from Jesus but from the more lurid of the early Old Testament writers) which has sought to proclaim that suffering is a punishment for sin, God's judgment on those who have done something wrong. The notion of God as a sort of bad-tempered wizard inflicting assorted woes on people who've annoyed him is as horrible as it's fantastic. But even if we could square this with a Christian view of God, and even if we can stomach the self-righteousness of it, the facts certainly won't support it. We know very well that when a disaster strikes it strikes everyone, guilty and innocent alike, and in areas no more deserving of punishment than anywhere else; and the people we know personally who have afflictions or handicaps of one kind or another are in no way more wicked than those who are not afflicted.

Equally mistaken, from the opposite point of view but for the same reason (self-righteousness), is the attitude which curses God because of the suffering of the innocent. This is more under-standable and less ungenerous, but it still reflects a very over-simplified view of God as well as a wrong one. But this is really another aspect of the same view which expects God to dish out lollipops as rewards for good behaviour. The author of psalm 4 had these things in the right perspective when he wrote that joy is a far greater gift than a good harvest.

Nevertheless many people do curse God (just as, in the beginning, we're told, Cain did) because they don't seem to be favoured; because they lose a loved one unexpectedly, or perhaps because they lead 'good' lives but are dogged by bad luck while others less righteous seem to do well. Life is not fair. But that's exactly the point. Life *is* not fair, a fact which writers, great observers of life, as different in philosophy as Hardy and Kipling have been at pains to point out. Life is not fair in any conventional sense, and there's nothing we can do about it. Life is not fair, nor have we been given any reason why it should be fair. Fairness is a chimera believed in by those who scorn the Church's teaching about envy and covetousness.

What is the answer? I really don't think there is one. As to the existence of suffering, it does seem to me that there would be not much point in the world without it; I mean, if the world were perfect it would be paradise already and what could it achieve? But I'm aware that this isn't much help, and doesn't begin to account for the way in which suffering is distributed. We can't account for the distribution of suffering, and it's futile to try. We just have to accept that suffering, as far as we can see indiscriminate, is part of the 'givenness' of the world. The only thing that can be said positively (and it's very little comfort) is that out of suffering much good frequently comes.

Now just a word about depression, for depression is an understandable by-product of suffering. – Understandable, but wrong. The Church has always taught that depression is a sin, and the reason is pretty obvious; depression is a symptom of loss of trust in God. If we look at another psalm, number 77 this time, we notice that it is in three sections. In the first section the poet is bitterly and despairingly recalling the great days of the past. In the second he remembers God, pauses, and regains his faith. In the third he again recalls the past, but this time in a mood not of despair but of confidence. Now the past has become a source of strength; God helped us before, he will help us again.

It seems to me that however we approach the problem we come back to faith. We must trust God. However terrible the things that happen, and however unfair they seem, we can do nothing but accept them (I'm talking of course about natural disasters, not man-made ones, and about bereavements and afflictions). That's the first thing. The second, in regard to our own afflictions, is to hope and believe that through suffering we may be purified and strengthened to carry out God's purposes. The third thing is for us, as Christians, to work for the relief of suffering, wherever, whenever, and however it occurs. And the fourth thing is for those of us who don't suffer very much to be thankful. But in the long run it is only through faith, however difficult and unreasonable, faith that in spite of the tragedies and perplexities of life, life is good and God is good, that we can remain sane and unembittered, and happy, as despite it all I'm convinced God means us to be.

Well, trust him or distrust him according to your temperament, but if you don't accept the fact that that is how life is, you will surely go mad with grief and frustration and self-pity.

Job had perfect trust in the beginning. Later he was led to doubt, but in the end returned to trust. Job was a blameless and godfearing man, not only doing no harm to anyone but actively doing good. Suddenly four separate disasters destroyed everything he had, including all his children. What is his reaction? He doesn't blame or curse God. He doesn't even question him. He simply thanks him for having allowed him to enjoy so many good things for so long. Such a trust, such a perfect acceptance of life as it comes, this is surely what we are to aim for. This is what Christianity, in the context of loving God, is all about. This is truly the faith that saves.

THE OYSTERCATCHER

There is a kind of loneliness which nothing can assuage, a black depression which simply takes hold of a person and cannot be shaken off until it is ready to go; no amount of company, however gay, however sincere, will do more than alleviate it temporarily. It is not a pathological condition (though there is a pathological condition with the same effect) – not a pathological condition,

95

because the recurrence of it ceases with the changing age or circumstances of the person afflicted.

Robert Short in *The Parables of Peanuts* tells of a teenage girl who had this trouble. Parents, friends, her own resources, could do nothing. She went to see the minister of her church, who told her there was nothing to be done; it was part of her growing pains, and would pass eventually; in the meantime she must bear it as best she could. She never went to church again.

A self-centred girl, rebuked for her self-centredness, blamed her troubles on the church rather than her own shortcomings.

Of course that is far too facile and hard-hearted a dismissal of the case. The girl had asked for spiritual help and was entitled to get it. The pastor had spoken the truth, no doubt as gently as he could, but the truth was insufficient.

A clergyman is very much at a disadvantage at these times. Pressed on the one hand by the inclination to say nothing at all (because there is nothing constructive to say) and on the other by the knowledge that he is bound to say something, he tries desperately to find the right thing to say only to discover that it is inevitably the wrong thing. In this case he tried to be comforting and said (quite truthfully) that it would pass. It's a pity that he wasn't able to say it tactfully enough to prevent her from making the situation worse. But how should he know? What is tact to one person is unctuousness to another. It is a very rare and gifted person indeed that can tell at a glance who needs to be bullied, who charmed, who treated frankly.

The trouble of course is that if you have a blanket put over your head and your arms tied, you don't stop to think that sooner or later somebody is going to loose you: you struggle.

THE
PARROT-FINCH

The parrot-finch, though very small, was a gay little thing – bright green and red like an animated Portuguese flag. He was fluttering about apparently inconsequentially, perhaps looking for something new, when his eye fell on the land-crab's hole. He didn't approach it directly, but perched now on one thing now on another, regarding it carefully from each different angle. After a while he began to get nearer to it each move. Eventually he stood right on the lip of it, peering within and cocking his head for any sound.

He was not an adventurous bird; in fact he was distinctly timid. One would not therefore have expected him to do other than fly away and leave the hole – wonderingly perhaps, but nonetheless leave it. But in fact he took a step forward and entered the hole. It was not only an uncharacteristic step, but seemed to him afterwards to have been an involuntary one. It was also a decisive step, evidently marking some kind of turning point in his life.

The tunnel sloped gently downwards and bore immediately to the right, so that the direct daylight was very soon cut off. Now it seemed there was something magical about this tunnel. It had started as just bare earth, roughly bored through and laboriously pushed to the surface. But it soon became (or so the parrot-finch fancied, or at any rate afterwards affirmed) a luxurious tunnel, completely sheathed in gleaming tiles, and with ingenious artificial lighting.

As soon as it finished sloping down, which was a long way from the entrance, and therefore at a great depth below the surface, it opened out into some kind of piazza so vast that the end and sides of it were, so to speak, beyond the horizon; – at all events, they were not to be seen. The roof was kept up, naturally enough, by a limitless forest of rather thick pillars. And every here and there, between four or more of these pillars, were little caverns, or the shops of a bazaar, or secret kiosks, or chantries, or cubicles – it was impossible at a glance to say what they were.

The parrot-finch walked round this enchanted place in fascination. Some of the caverns were enticing, and he only failed to enter from fear of missing something even more wonderful. Others were thrilling to contemplate only, he felt, at a distance. From others he recoiled. Still others left him with a delightful sense of mystery which it seemed it would be a pity to destroy by exploring. And yet he didn't really understand the promise of any of them.

During his rapt amble he forgot all about time and place and circumstance. So it was with rather a shock that suddenly, as he came round a corner, he caught sight, several caverns away, of the land-crab. He was immediately terrified. A land-crab is an ugly and forbidding creature. Its vast head and mouth, separate bulbs of eyes, and evil scurrying motion, might be designed not just to frighten but to horrify.

And so the bird skipped back round the corner and stood panting with his back to the wall. He looked round to find his way back to the tunnel, but the view was identical in each direction, and he had walked so in circles and zigzags that it was impossible to tell which way he had come. What should he do? If only, he thought, he had brought a friend with him; they could work something out together, or at least things wouldn't seem so bad. In a panic he moved off as fast as he could, blindly hoping that by some chance he was going in the right direction. He knew nothing about land-crabs, but instinct told him to keep as far away as possible. After a little while he got some control of himself, and kept his eyes open, looking back to see if he was followed, looking in all directions when he got to a crossway. From time to time he saw the land-crab, and then would change direction and move off again with renewed speed.

The land-crab, for his part, had been even more astonished than the bird at the initial encounter. It seemed an appealing creature, that bird, so small, so brightly coloured, so shy and harmless-looking. But suspicious instinct told him that that was just the sort of creature to beware of. The land-crab had powerful jaws and limbs, and was well able to defend himself against very much stronger enemies than the parrot-finch, yet the custom of his kind was to destroy anything which appeared to threaten – and anything unfamiliar apparently did threaten. So he obeyed his urge and stalked the bird, intending absolutely to catch him and kill him and so find security again.

The chase went on a long time, till both creatures were dizzy. Arriving at the same corner at the same time from different directions, they met with considerable force. In their mutual semi-concussed state the natural good manners of both of them reappeared. Each helped the other to his feet, and they found each other charming.

THE PARTRIDGE

If you have no friends you grow attached to your possessions. I knew no one but my owner, who was unable to spend a lot of time with me. I made a sort of friend of the pear tree which grew in his garden, and spent all my time sitting in it. My owner wanted to give me to his beloved as a Christmas present. Because he was kind and sensitive he dug up the pear tree and presented us both to her.

THE PEACOCK

The peacock raised his head and listened. He could hear nothing, however, so he bent down to the ground again and went on searching for food. Every morning he came out on to the front drive and paced up and down it, from time to time stopping to stretch himself erect as though to remind anyone who happened to be looking that he was one of the beauties of this park of beauties, and from time to time bowing swiftly to snatch a beetle from the dust. The drive was a good place for beetles, especially, for some reason, at the point where it divided. – It forked into two, each part swinging round in a great arc to meet in front of the steps leading up to the terrace.

Again the peacock lifted his head to listen. It was time the princess was out. Every morning at a certain hour she came out on to the terrace to play, and the first thing she did was to run across the terrace to the balustrade and look for the peacock, and then the peacock would move at his sedate invariable walk towards the steps and up them to the terrace. They played together always, these two, for the princess had no other companion, and the peacock too was alone of his kind in the park. Whenever the princess was out of doors, whether in the gardens or down by the lake, the peacock would follow her. Often she would run ahead, eager to see what was round the next corner, but the peacock would never increase his pace. Then she would run back and throw her arms round his neck, and then be off again as fast as her long dresses would allow her.

The peacock listened hard. She ought definitely to be there by now. He stretched his neck to try and see the terrace, but it was much too high for him to see beyond the balustrade. It was also very broad, the terrace, so that the palace, which was only two storeys high, could not be seen at all from down below, until one had gone quite a long way down the drive away from it. He looked at the sun; it was well up in the sky. What could be keeping her? He decided to go and meet her, and proceeded with his usual deliberate but unself-conscious dignity to the steps, which he mounted one by one, all the hundred and eighty of them, past the smaller terraces on either hand of carefully tended flower beds, eyeing the enormous urns that marked the summit of his ascent.

When he got to the top he flew on to one of the urns and sat there for some minutes scanning the house and all its windows for any sign of life. It was a long low edifice with a flat roof and an even skyline broken only by the extra storey in the middle three bays; this storey was a sham in fact – just a stone façade with nothing behind. There were thirty-one bays in all. Each one was separated from the next by a composite column – Ionic rams' horns springing from Corinthian foliage. These columns were large and square and flat – barely projecting from the façade – except the four which framed the three middle bays, and these were round and free-standing and more slender. Each bay contained a large French window on the lower floor and another on the upper; those on the upper floor each gave on to a little balcony protected by a wrought iron rail – flat in the twenty-eight outer bays but bowed in the three middle ones.

The peacock was uncertain what to do. Never before had he looked for the princess; always she had come to the balustrade when he had expected her, and that had been that. Eventually he flew down again to the flagstones of the terrace and started pacing over to the corner of the palace on his left, where, he knew, was the French window of her drawing room.

When he got there he walked right up to the window and stared through it, his eye to the glass. There was nobody there, no sign of anybody. The still within was so absolute that it felt as though at any moment it would explode, as though the objects in the room could stand the utter inaction for not a moment longer, as though everything were poised on the edge of an earthquake. The peacock moved on along the front of the house, staring into each window for a moment as he passed. It was alike in every room: no trace of life, the same explosive stillness. Chairs with legs of gilded curls waited for some signal to fly upwards, tapestries to fall apart, china statues to disintegrate, chandeliers to drop to the floor like the rain of summer storms, silver vessels to hurtle through the air, curtains to collapse, plaster scrolls to crack like burning apple wood. Heavy with the sense of life suspended, the house appeared to be waiting for the kiss of some enchanted rider to restore its animation, and the peacock had to remind himself that it was only yesterday and not a hundred years ago that laughter and wine and the busy silence of servants had been in every room.

Arrived finally at the other end of the front, he paused for a moment, and then turned to his left and made towards the stables. Past these, he turned again to his left, and so came into the meander garden, which was not very aptly named for all the paths were straight. There were dozens of them, all at right angles and diagonals, each one bordered by little square-cut hedges two feet high, with roses planted in the beds they protected. Here the princess often walked, lost in her own thoughts, the peacock following, a stately small procession. Today the peacock picked his way alertly through a series of paths, keeping the house as much as possible on his left, his eyes glancing here and there to catch a glimpse of the princess.

He turned to his left a third time, passing the servants' wing of the house. Up to now the only feeling roused in him by the princess' absence had been one of irritation that she had not appeared at the usual time, but now he began to feel some alarm. Without his realizing it she had become to an enormous extent part of his life. He had not before had occasion to contemplate the prospect of life without her, and now that he did this prospect was uninviting. – Not that it occurred to him that the princess was actually gone; it was just that for the first time she was not there when he expected her to be, and he missed her. And so he was very slightly alarmed, with a presentiment of possibly being without her again at times in the future, as he turned left yet a forth time and found himself on the terrace where he had started.

He began a second circuit of the house, his pace increasing. His annoyance vanished rapidly as his alarm grew. From somewhere against the inside of his backbone a feeling of something cold and heavy and deadening started to spread through his body to his mind, gripping it, filling it with an icy voidlike dread. As he walked he looked in every hopeless corner, reason gradually departing.

He completed his second circuit and began the third without noticing it. Now panic seized him and he flew quite blindly round the house, seeing nothing but its oppressive mocking walls which shut him out, kept him from the princess, seemed to dance forward and back sniggering and to fold themselves round him like a ring of bullying children round a victim, holding hands, circling, screaming, hostile, inescapable, nightmarish.

By the time he reached his starting point once again he was exhausted, and flopped down on the flagstones heaving and staring. Gradually the flood of terror receded, leaving only a numbing emptiness. He knew now that the princess was gone for good, that she whose companionship was the essence of his life had left his life, that life as he had known it was no more.

He got to his feet and wandered once more round the house. He was no longer looking for her, but partly aimless, partly aware that life must go on, and just a little, in a far corner of his mind, dimly conscious that if he could only contain his heart long enough time would dull the ache.

This time when he got to the servants' wing he did not turn left and return to the terrace, but strolled off into the park. There were paths which led in many directions through the flowering bushes, and he followed a succession of these without noticing in which direction they were taking him until he came to an open space at the top of a small cliff overlooking a lake. There was a railing at the edge, and here he perched for a while looking out over the lake.

The lake was an ornamental one, made artificially by partially damming the end of the shallow valley, and its banks had been elegantly landscaped and provided with the features appropriate to such a conceit – ruins, pagodas, oriental bridges, a dozen such toys. This lake and its surroundings had been the favourite place of the princess, and so it was with real if somewhat self-conscious pain that the peacock remembered times passed in that place, staring, between the sardonic branches of a withered tree clinging to the cliff-top, at each of its exotic features in turn.

But he was too restless to stay there long. To the left of the railing a tiny stream splashed over the cliff into the water below; to the right a footpath had been cut, which zigzagged its way down the precipice to the lakeside. Down this he now progressed, until, arrived at the bottom, he began a slow sentimental tour of the lakeshore, torturing himself with melancholy perversity by recalling the haunts and foibles of the girl who had been his playmate.

Here was a carved stone bench on which she had often sat, here an almond tree the petals of whose blossom she had gathered in handfuls and scattered and gathered again, here a temple whose Grecian steps had been her stage for posturing, gracefully, laughingly, deprecatingly, while the peacock displayed himself between the pillars. In one bay the land shelved into the water so gently that it was only ankle deep some distance from the edge, and here the landscapist had caused to be scattered some boulders and a quantity of smaller stones to make a romantic rocky shore. On one of these boulders the princess would lie with her fingers in the water and her long hair falling round her face.

Just above the point where the little river that formed it entered the lake was a ruined water-mill. It was not a real water-mill; that is to say it had never worked, but had been built as a ruin, erected complete with missing planks and a wheel that did not quite reach the water. Nevertheless it was a place of atmosphere. Since no one else from the palace ever bothered to visit it, as they did the temples and pagodas, it had always been a private place for the princess and the peacock. He entered it, not in the least expecting to see her, for even the most hopeless hope had long since left him, yet scarcely able to believe that he could be alone there. The air was heavy with her presence. The tide of bereavement, condoned self-pity, rose again in his throat, choking him. In agony he stretched his neck with a great harsh cry that shook the brittle rafters of the mill only to be drowned by the chattering water. Defeated, he left.

Down the far side of the lake he went, through the grotto with its window just above the water level, where the young princess would daydream of the end of mighty voyages – ships from the Indies dropping anchor in the roads outside – or all an afternoon sit watching the endless rods of rain piercing the passive surface of the water.

A sidetrack led away from the lake, up a hill and then across a sunken road, carried by a bridge of jagged stones. It led to the dower house. This was another ruin, but a genuine one. Ages before it had had a life of its own, but now for many years it had stood unwanted. The ornamental urns were overturned, little sycamores grew between the slabs of the steps, the terrace was a jungle of valerian, one leaf of the front door was missing.

After staring at it awhile with his mind elsewhere the peacock was turning to go when a sudden movement amongst the valerian caught his eye. He watched but saw nothing more. Carefully he walked towards the place, and as he got there was able to trace a wave of movement through the leaves, which he followed till he found himself at the door. After pausing at the gloom he stepped inside, and felt a pat on the back of his leg. He sprang round, but found nothing. After a minute he heard a little laughing squeak, apparently from somewhere above him; turning with the utmost speed he just caught a movement between the banisters of the staircase. He was cautiously climbing the stairs when something landed beside him and, brushing past, disappeared round the corner. He went back to the hall and waited. Again he felt a pat on his leg, and this time saw something scurrying into one of the rooms. The room was furnished. Evidently it had been the dining room, for in the middle was an oval table surrounded by chairs. The peacock walked round the room, peering behind the sideboards and cabinets, listening hard. Everything was covered with dust and with cobwebs which caught the odd rays of light penetrating the rotten shutters. His eyes were accustomed to this curious twilight by now, and when he felt a pat on his head he looked round sharply and was able to recognize his will-o'-the-wisp.

Sitting on one of the dining-room chairs, her head on one side and smiling cheekily, was a kitten. She jumped down and began a crazy game, flinging herself this way and that, over and under the peacock, somersaulting, dancing, swinging, flying through the air. The peacock found himself joining in involuntarily.

They played together thus for some time, and then stopped, panting, and rested. The kitten wonderingly stroked the peacock's neck; the peacock gently explored with his beak the furrow down the kitten's forehead. Together they walked out on to the terrace. For ten minutes the peacock had forgotten to think of the princess. The sun was shining brilliantly.

THE
PELICAN

There is a little town on the west coast to which in the old days very few strangers used to come, for at that time there was no convenient way into it. It was a pleasant and easy-going place, full of sunshine, lemon trees, hard-baked red houses, and wandering pigs.

To the south of the town was a beach of soft sand. This beach was furnished with nothing beyond a simple hut, from which a moustachioed gentleman dispensed drinking coconuts and light-hearted wisdom. At the back of the beach was the jungle. Just off the beach, disposed in the water (which was shallow for very few yards and then descended abruptly), were several boulders.

On one of these boulders a large brown pelican sat all day once, motionless and with closed eyes. For much of the morning a noisy group of youngsters splashed round the boulder and mocked him, evidently at a loss to know why any creature should want to sit silent and alone. The pelican gave no sign of noticing them. When they went home to lunch he hadn't moved at all.

In the afternoon a solitary man came to the beach. He seemed to recognize something in the pelican that he understood, and more that he would like to understand. He trod water beside the pelican's rock for a long time. Some kind of comprehension of an inner completeness seemed to transmit itself between them. But when the man left the water the pelican still hadn't moved.

Later another group of cheerful folk arrived to play. They too stared and laughed at the enigmatic bird, but failed to stir him. It was only when the sun had disappeared in to the water that he opened his eyes and yawned, and with a contemptuous glance at the people surrounding him flew unhurriedly towards where the sun had been.

THE PENGUIN

'E, se mais mundo houvera, lá chegara.'
   Camões, *Os Lusíadas* (canto vii)

The emperor penguins have an unusual breeding cycle. While the male fasts and incubates the egg the female goes off on a combination of grand tour and retreat. Later they change places. The adolescent birds get together in groups when the Spring thaw approaches, and when the ice they are standing on breaks off they let it carry them wherever the current takes it. A poet has written of these:

.... birds
Like noblemen with gout and goitre
That patiently await
The strange fulfilment of an endless destiny;
Or in the soft grey young days go

Breasting into the unknown
On a hope-shaped scrap of floe.

One wonders if perhaps their feelings are similar to those of astronauts, who fare out into space hundreds of thousands of miles from security, driven by some urge which they seem unable satisfactorily to account for. The things that catch the imagination about space are its newness and its mathematics – the immensity of its distances compared with those we are accustomed to. But inconceivably courageous as the astronauts are, they have, if you look at the matter coldly, two advantages which the early navigators did not have; notwithstanding the distances, they are only away a matter of days, and they are never out of audial contact with their base.

From time to time the desire to find God (or some beyondmost, call it what you will) becomes a compulsion which seizes whole peoples and drives them to prolonged activity of one kind or another – for the glory of God. In medieval Europe it took the form of building ever higher and more elaborate cathedrals. By the beginning of the fifteenth century a different mania began to take hold of the Portuguese: an urge to roam the unknown seas and complete the map of the world. In the wake of the navigators came military and commercial enterprises which so small a nation had no hope of maintaining in their entirety. But even as distant lands were being settled, the navigators were discovering others yet more distant. For two hundred years the expeditions went on, and so many voyages naturally begot a number of wrecks; the cost to Portugal's manpower was enormous. Pessoa wrote of this in *Mar Português*, of the orphaned and the son-deprived, of all the maidens who married men they didn't love because their lovers lay with the sea, of how pain is the cost of anything the soul can worthily achieve and he who would sail beyond Cape Bojador must be content to suffer pain.

The Infante Henrique sent out his first navigator, João de Trasto, in 1415. In 1420 João Gonçalvez Zarco discovered Madeira. In 1427 Diogo de Sevill explored the Azores, and Gonçalo Velho Cabral did the same more thoroughly in 1431. It was in 1434 that Gil Eannes became the first to sail beyond Cape Bojador. Diniz Diaz rounded Cape Verde in 1445, and the following year Alvaro Fernandez passed the Bissagos, while one year later again Nuno Tristão discovered Guinea. In 1455 Alvise

Cadamosto explored the lower reaches of the Senegal and Gambia rivers, and the following year he discovered the Cape Verde Islands. Pedro de Sintra reached Sierra Leone in 1462. During the 1470s Fernão Gomes opened up the coast from Cape Palmas to Cape St. Catherine. Diogo Cão discovered and explored the Congo in 1484. Only three years later Bartolemeu Dias doubled the Cape of Good Hope. In 1497 Vasco da Gama discovered the sea route to India and explored, cursorily, the East African coast, reaching Bombay in 1498. Meanwhile Pedro Cavilhão had set out from Portugal in 1487 on a land and sea voyage crossing the Isthmus of Suez; he discovered, among other places, Ethiopia (in 1490), Aden, Socotra, and the sea route into the Persian Gulf. Ascension and St. Helena were discovered by João da Nova in 1501 and 1502, while Tristão da Cunha found his island in 1506. Pedro Mascarenhas discovered Mauritius in 1505, and Lorenzo Almeida Madagascar in 1506. Francisco de Almeida landed in Ceylon in 1505. In 1509 Diogo Lopez de Seguiera cruised the west coast of Malaya, discovering both Sumatra and Java; the East Indies were further explored by Antonio d'Abreu, who sighted New Guinea in 1511. In the same year Duarte Fernandes was sent to establish relations with Siam, Fernão Pires de Andrade arrived in Canton in 1517, and finally Mendez Pinto became the first European to visit Japan in 1537.

In the meantime other Portuguese navigators were going in the opposite direction. Within months of the Genoese's stumbling on the Bahamas, possibly even before, João Fernão de Lavrador was in the Gulf of St. Lawrence. Duarte Pacheco Pereira evidently found South America in 1498 or 1499, and in 1500 Pedrálvarez Cabral discovered Brazil. Also that year Gaspar Cortereal cruised the coast of Greenland and rediscovered Labrador. Fernão de Magelhães, in the course of his voyage round the World, and approaching from the East, discovered both Guam and the Philippines in 1521. It was not until the first year of the seventeenth century that a European set eyes on Australia; Manoel Godinho de Eredia discovered it in 1601. 'And were there more lands to discover they would be there too'.

Such was Portugal's contribution to the history of endeavour. One can imagine them after weeks, months, of empty sea, straining their eyes for a sight of some new land – some of the lower ranks perhaps still not convinced that the World wasn't flat with an edge they would all sail over into Hades. Or in some strange tropic estuary, staring mildly over the side with their courtly curious faces at the banks so different from those they had left, ages past it would seem, in Portugal.

THE PEREGRINE

One peregrine had been run over. The corpse lay on the road, flattened, recognizable only by a few wing feathers. The other, the mate, stood, solitary and still, beside the melancholy remnant. Cars used the road. As each approached the mate rose into the air, and, when it had passed, alighted again to continue the vigil. This continued until the heavy tyres of tractors had dispersed the last of the remains.

THE PHEASANT

It was a fourth-rate aviary in the grimy park of a small provincial town, but it boasted a pheasant house. As is well-known, there are many varieties of pheasant in the world, some of them most exotically plumed. But of the twelve or fifteen birds in this collection there was only one that was not a common pheasant; she was a Lady Amherst.

The manner of this bird was strikingly different from that of the others: not affected in any way, but naturally pleasing and gracious. Some of the common pheasants didn't like this at all, and accused her of 'being stuck up' or of 'putting on airs'; they said that, since it was immoral for some to have been brought up differently from others, she deserved to suffer and ought to be ostracized. Others recognized that it was natural, simply a matter of different background and did their best to make her feel at home, finding it a shame for her that she couldn't be among those whom she understood and who understood her.

She herself did her best to be at home, and was certainly friendly to everyone. But to lower deliberately the standards she'd been taught at all costs to preserve was something beyond her. Till the day of her death she was recognizably apart.

THE
PHOEBE

One would have thought she was one of the best-set-up creatures in society as regards friends. She had been through just the right number of divorces, patronized the right slimming farms, visited the right resorts at the right seasons. Her cocktail comments were untrite enough to pass for wit but sufficiently obviously unoriginal to save her from being considered eccentric. Her face was lifted but not astronomically. She was animated without being so gay as to appear vulgar.

She played bridge every Thursday afternoon, canasta on alternate Monday evenings, and (a little dubiously) sometimes whist on Saturdays. On Tuesdays in the season she attended subscription concerts. On Sundays she would often drive into the country and spend the day with one or another polite acquaintance, with whom she shared the mutual self-deception that the use of Christian names made them intimate. Wednesday was the day of her luncheon group and her keep-fit club. And on Fridays she nearly always had one or two friends to dinner.

A full life it would seem. None of her friends ever perceived that, full as it was, it wasn't full enough. Whenever she returned to her apartment, or whenever she shut the door behind the last of her guests, she was left with a sense of unfillable emptiness.

THE PIGEON

Of the huge blocks that divide cities up into little dark canyons of humanity, some seem to be clean and almost sterilely shining, as though the breezes they meet carry only the cleansing rain. Others are overlaid with dirt, seeming to attract all the fumes and particles and wind-blown mud that float about the city seeking a resting place. It is the same with the city birds. There are sleek and glowing pigeons that ornament the shiny buildings or perch fastidiously and incongruously on a corner of the dirty ones. And there are grimy nondescript pigeons who appear to catch all the ill winds blowing.

In one city the largest of all the downtown office blocks is more arresting in its drabness even than in its size, rising out of the street like a squalid cliff. Sometimes a little after noon a thin line of sun will creep along the gutter and lie all squint-mouthed, pawing the building like a badly-treated puppy desperate for affection; that is the nearest it ever gets to the real light of day. Its windowsills in particular are heaped with filth of every kind. On one of these windowsills, some twenty or thirty floors up, there used to live a pigeon whose condition was in harmony with that of the building.

She was small, thin, bedraggled, almost bald in patches, with a squint, a crossed beak, and one leg shorter than the other. She was also not very intelligent. Perhaps as a result of these things, perhaps by coincidence, she never had any companions. As a result of that she had ceased trying to keep up appearances – if indeed she ever had tried. When hunger compelled her she would go and root about in a slovenly manner for essential food; otherwise she just sat on the windowsill rocking about in a hopeless sort of way.

In the normal course of events no other bird ever used that windowsill. But it chanced one day that a travelling pigeon stopped to rest on it in passing. And having stopped he was unable to go on. He collapsed into the corner, apparently more dead than alive.

The other pigeon, once recovered from her surprise, was quite bewildered; but once recovered from her bewilderment she went to see what she could do for him. In the event he was ill for a long time, but she, having never before had anything to show concern or affection for, nursed him devotedly. He was sincerely grateful for her care.

He was a nasty little bird really; a cheap, slick, whiny sort of character, as thin and mean as she was, though in better case both mentally and physically. But he came to love her; and she, who had never been loved, came to love him with utter singlemindedness.

On the first night after he had really recovered they went uptown together. In the centre of the gayest part of the city is a large square with several fountains which continually change their shape and on which coloured lights play. The two birds wandered together amongst these marvels. There is also in the square a statue on a column, standing in a pose once considered heroic, with one hand outstretched. The moon caused the statue to cast a shadow, and this shadow together with the optical tricks played by the constant shifting of the lights and the water brought about a strange illusion. For one instant it appeared as if a godlike being was patting the heads of the biggest and most golden birds in all creation.

THE PIPIT

Every day that hot August the alpine pipit saw the man setting out on his solitary walks and returning at dusk. The thing she remarked about him was a radiant peacefulness.

Some days he would walk downstream past the sawmill to the kingcup fields. Some days he would walk upstream into the cool woods, where there was a gallery of rock overlooking the waterfall. Sometimes he would loiter the whole day among the autumn crocuses (which in spite of their name bloomed at the top of summer). Sometimes he would cross the valley and stroll hazelnutted footpaths, or sit in the slanting meadows. Other times he went up higher and strode for miles through the pine forests. Occasionally he would ascend the bare steep slopes on the near side of the valley, and let the keen air blow about his body.

If she had asked him perhaps he would have said that he belonged to some strange pantheistic sect which worships God on mountains.

THE PLOVER

The reeds in silence shiver at the morning;
Behind the blackthorns grey the scudding clouds;
From each despondent clump of grass
The luckless plover flies.

– And have we met before?
In April fields beyond the death of time,
In green and white and palest early gold,
In joy before the pain of parting innocence,
Oh, have we met before?

(The promises God makes to little children
Are broken by the bureaucratic fates.)

The frosted ploughland smoulders in the twilight;
The stream malingers through the aching dust;
The sloes drop one by one by one;
The fading primrose dies.

– Yes, in the country, long ago,
When all was golden from the spring of day

Till night came softly by the willowed ponds our world,
You came one afternoon along the Hills,
And stayed,
And shortly went away . . .
Yes, in the country, long ago.

(But the cruellest fond remembrance
Is, oh, better than a void.)

THE
POOR-WILL

The sum of the songs
Of the loneliness of poverty
Trilling from tree to tree
In the badlands
East of Eden
Symphonies
A togethering of the rejectable.

THE POPINJAY

The popinjay had a bee in his bonnet about vanity. It was his contention that all the evils of this world are brought about by vanity of one form or another – indeed, that in the long run, directly or indirectly, vanity is the biggest driving power of all the emotions and has more influence on events than love and fear combined.

He had a little to say about loneliness in this connection, and here it is:

'Loneliness too can be the result of vanity. For loneliness is caused not so much by being alone as by a sense of exclusion, and to feel excluded is bound to be wounding to the vanity. And some people feel themselves to be inadequate if they are apparently unable to acquire a companion. Many dislike being alone because they're afraid that others will look down on them if they have no companion. This is very understandable, but pure vanity.

'Loneliness is something we must all have experienced at one time or another, and therefore we should be able to identify ourselves with the loneliness of others. Yet I'm very much afraid that far, far more people than we dream of suffer from chronic loneliness.'

THE
PROTONOTARY

The cardinal, the protonotary, and the friar, agreed to preach on the same text from the day's epistle: Ephesians, ch.4, v.25. The protonotary spoke as follows:

'"We are members one of another". If you can imagine this in diagrammatic form, think of yourself as a dot, and from that dot a lot of lines go out in every direction, to other dots which represent all the people we know. And from each of those dots other lines go out to still other dots, which are all the people *they* know, and so on. It's an incredibly complex picture. And because life is a matter of relationships and we are members one of another, our relations with each person we know will influence our relations with each other person we know. We may know, for example, X, and Y, and Z; this means that our view of X will be influenced, perhaps to a large extent or perhaps to a small extent, but certainly and inevitably influenced, by Y's view of X and by Z's view of X. Et cetera, et cetera. It will also of course be influenced by our own temperament and by the special circumstances of our acquaintance with each other person, but this is beside the point; the point is that all our relationships interact upon one another.

'On the other hand, consider loneliness. Loneliness comes not necessarily from solitude but always, I think, from a sense of exclusion. We must all have experienced this feeling – when having just moved to a new place, or started a new job or a new school, or even at a party where we don't know anybody else. – All the dots are connected to one another by a network of lines and just the dot which represents us is unconnected, cut off from the network. Very soon (how soon depends on our own friendliness and on that of the others) the connections will be made and we shall be taken into the network.

'God is much concerned in all this. Just as our relationship with each person we know affects our relationship with each other person we know, so our relationship with each person we know affects our relationship with God, and our relationship with God affects all our relationships with people. This is pretty obvious. As for the Church, the Church is the great body of Christians, who claim to obey God's will and to follow the way of Christ (which is the same thing). If the Church were perfect every dot would be joined to every other dot.'

THE PUFFIN

For many years I used to go annually to the same islet off the ocean coast. It was just by the entrance to a bay containing a fishermen's village. This village was an entity very much at one with its surroundings, for the houses seemed to have grown naturally from the serpentine of which and on which they were built, and gave the impression that the rough salt winds were exactly the kind of air they needed to breathe. Grass was the only thing that grew among the houses, and it too was short and tough and grey-green, cropping out between the stone wherever it seemed appropriate.

The people of the village became familiar to me by sight, and there were two in particular whose lives fascinated me. One was a little girl; I suppose she must have been nine or ten when I first saw her. The other was an old man.

He, like every man in the village, had been a fisherman in his youth and prime, but that had been a very long time before. As he grew older he had left the fishing fleet and done odd jobs on the shore, but that too had been long ago, and now in his old age he had taken with a fierce energy to some kind of craft. Always a solitary man, after his wife's death he had turned even more away from the life of the village. He became, some said, rather peculiar. The boys made fun of him, and he shunned people more and more. Eventually he became stone deaf and always more suspicious, and then ceased to leave the house at all. Any callers he would chase away with ferocious rage. By the time I knew him he was thus ancient, isolated, and only interested in his craft.

The girl was a villager. Her father and older brothers were fishermen, and her older sisters were married to fishermen. But she seemed to have little interest in the doings of other children. Most of her time she spent with the old man, and she was the only person he would allow into the house.

They never spoke, but obviously felt no need to. It was she who kept his house neat, and who prepared his meals. The households in the village all took a share in providing food and drink for him (as they did for all the old people who had no family). And each day someone gave the girl a shilling tobacco money for the two of them (in those days a shilling went a long way in a tobacconist's) which she would scrupulously divide, spending three quarters of it on tobacco for his pipe and the rest on her own cigarettes. Her mother allowed her to take whatever she needed in the way of cleaning materials.

Every day after school she collected what supplies were needed and made her way up the lane to his house. She would make up the fire, do some cleaning, tidy the whole house, cook his tea, and wash the dishes. Then she would sit at the kitchen table and do her homework, read, watch him at work, or simply daydream. When it grew late she would go home. Through all this he gave no sign of noticing that she was there, yet both seemed quite content with things as they were.

The relationship persisted for a good many years. But eventually doubts seemed to gather in the old man's disordered mind, suspicions, perhaps, that she was sent to spy by the rest of mankind, whose aim, he believed, was to persecute him. He became more and more restless when she was there, stared at her, and toyed with heavy objects. One evening the torment in him boiled over, and he drove her away.

She went as she had stayed, in silence. As she walked down the hill the wind dried the hint of moisture in her eyes.

THE
QUAIL

The cages were like so many shoe boxes piled in orderly fashion on a shelf, one deep but ten high and a dozen broad. They were only open to the light at the far end; ceilings, floors, walls, were solid. The near end was also solid, but with in each case a door opening on to the corridor which ran along the length of each storey. (Actually 'cages' is the wrong word, for in reality the inhabitants were naturally perfectly free to come and go as they pleased; it just seemed as if they were penned up.)

The quail got home and tried to settle down to something. He always found it very hard. It wasn't that he was bored, or restless, or lacking in inner resources. It was simply that he seemed so alone, so unbelonging in this place. He couldn't concentrate. He found himself listening all the time to the other inmates of the building as they came in and out (they never seemed to talk, so perhaps they didn't know one another any better than he knew any of them). There was one coming now. He waited till the steps passed his door, then started counting. One, two ... ten ... twenty ... thirty ... thirty-seven; then a scrape, a click, and a slam. Number fourteen was home.

Every evening he heard number fourteen come home. He had no idea what he looked like; he'd never seen him, only heard those footsteps every twenty-four hours. He'd seen very few of those who lived in the flats, and never one close enough to smile at. This complete lack of communication in his immediate surroundings seemed to make life a fragmented affair altogether.

Every evening he contemplated getting up, resolutely opening his door, striding down the corridor, knocking on a door – any door – and saying heartily: 'I'm so-and-so. I thought it was time we got acquainted'. But he never did. He couldn't quite make out if it was pride or timidity, fear of being rebuffed or fear of being thought a fool. But in any case he could never bring himself to do it.

Every evening it was the same. The same loneliness, the same indecision, the same failure to do anything constructive, the same misery, the same eventual crawling into bed wondering what it was all about.

THE QUARRION

Opportunism.
Dedication.
Fulfilment.
The chance that makes the choice
Of good and evil.

Take Eichmann and take Gandhi.
Gandhi a German in the early 'forties
Might have slaughtered Jews,
Eichmann in India
Been frail and saintly all his days.

THE RAVEN

When he got to his new school the raven wasn't very happy. The others seemed to take a delight in teasing him, insulting him, generally showing contempt for him, and (worst of all) excluding him as far as possible from their activities. For the most part this didn't last, but there remained a little of it throughout his time there.

Years afterwards he realized that the reason for his unpopularity was the fact that he had been a peculiarly unpleasant adolescent. That didn't matter any more. What shamed him was the recollection that he had himself taken an eager part in the victimization of others who were unpopular, – he who had known so well the loneliness and despair of being unpopular. Presumably it had been a desire to curry popularity by openly siding with the mob.

The puzzling thing was that though he himself had not been likeable, many of those the mob took against were, though perhaps hardly charming, pleasant enough. All his life he wondered about this, but he never found an answer.

THE REDSTART

A number of redstarts flirted with ism. Most of them gave it up in the end, and because they were questing and intelligent birds someone had the idea of inviting them along to the studio together and making a programme of their comments. Each one in turn was asked why he had rejected ism.

The first one said: 'I don't like systems. I thought perhaps this system was different, and anyway it was worth investigating, but it's a very systematic system. There is little room for an individual in a system, and the more systematic a system the less room there is for the individual.'

The second one said: 'I believe in the soul.'

The third one said: 'That's interesting. I would prefer to say I believe in the spirit. With ism everything physical and material is taken care of but the spirit is ignored. There is no place for endeavour. I've come to believe that we have a need of decisions to make, of people, or things, or ideas, to care for and to care about. Even our tribulations are a necessary part of life. It is not enough to leave everything to a superpaternal state. If we do, life, however comfortable it may be, becomes a mere existence.'

The fourth one said: 'It seems to me now that no secular religion, however gentle and considerate, can ever be wholly satisfactory. They all, by definition, start from the worth of bird, or the dignity of bird, or the rights of bird, or some such phrase. They are egocentric. They cannot therefore teach humility, and humility seems to me to be the thing we are missing out on. Only humility can be saving. In other words salvation, as I see it, lies in giving oneself, not in getting for oneself. But the secular religions aim (with laudable intent, obviously) to get things for bird. And then again I can't help feeling there's a basic arrogance in birdism. (Birdism seems to be a pretty popular creed these days, and it's surely the basis of ism and other similar philosophies.) Birdism virtually makes a God of Bird. But what grounds have we got (other than self-interest and self-satisfaction) for assuming that the world exists for the benefit of bird?'

The fifth one said: 'It's a question of exploitation. In the old days, we're led to believe, the masses were exploited and a handful did the exploiting. Doubtless this is true, and it was a shameful thing. Nowadays we're all exploiters. We exploit upwards and downwards and sideways. And not only is this accepted, but those who can't manage to exploit are looked on as failures. Well, I thought ism would be different. And ideally it probably is. But I soon found that in practice ism is too often a cultivation which serves the vanity of the leaders. They exploit you for all you're worth, and if you're not worth anything to them they get rid of you as economically as possible.'

The sixth one said: 'Ism is concerned with ideas about birds. It has no concern whatever for birds themselves.'

The seventh one said: 'I thought it would be an end to loneliness. And in the beginning it was. There is an immense comradeship in striving together towards a goal. But once the aim was achieved our common purpose was gone, and it seemed we had no more use for one another.'

THE REEVE

Buttoned and belted in an ancient mackintosh,
Hair blown autumnly across her shoulder,
She walked unnoticing past still façades
And the interluded heaps of rubble.

Standing a moment at the corner,
She saw the shadow of a carriage pass
Bearing herself
To some reception in another age.

She turned, sighing a little quickly,
And her footsteps died away into silence.

THE RIFLEMAN

The rifleman arrived, with others of his kind individually, at the depot towards evening. Of exclusive and somewhat refined upbringing, he had all along been very nervous of this encounter and of the subsequent co-habitation, but felt it was something which must be done and would prove worthwhile later, a necessary prelude to the fulfilment of his modest ambitions. Well, the encounter had now been made, and it was just a question of enduring a strange and cruder way of life for as long as would prove necessary.

On arrival he (like the others) was handed some equipment for the night and led to a hut, where he was assigned a resting place – all without comment. In the morning they were told to get up, they were fed, they were stood in rows, they were handed more equipment, they were stood in rows again, fed again, stood in rows again, marched from place to place, and left standing in rows. From time to time those who gave the orders talked to one another, but never to them. Questions received a not unkindly but always non-comittal answer. In the evening they were fed again and sent back to their hut.

This went on for several days. Then one afternoon they were stood in rows and marched off several miles to another hut. They lived in this hut for a week or more, still carrying out the same programme (or lack of programme) as before. But one day they were marched back to the original hut. Again the daily ritual was resumed. They never saw anybody but one another and those who gave the immediate orders.

The rifleman began to get to know his fellows. Some of them, though from a different background, found the crudeness of the remainder as distasteful as he did. The remainder, the crude ones, he discovered were for the most part pretty good fellows; it was hardly their fault if they didn't bother about the niceties of a way of life they had never been instructed in. He was surprised to find himself, not exactly at home, but certainly on pleasant enough terms of comradeship.

Still the baffling lack of purpose in their existence persisted. From time to time they got glimpses of distant figures scurrying about as though they at least had a purpose, but these were people from another life; they never approached, let alone spoke to them. One had a feeling of being utterly forgotten, that here one was and here one would stay, a group of people who had apparently been dropped right out of the pattern of things.

And then one morning, after they had eaten, they were stood in rows and marched away as usual. But this time they were taken somewhere new. They stopped outside a row of offices and were told to sit down. One by one they were called in to one or other of the offices. When the rifleman's turn came he found himself talking at great length to a kind and knowledgeable and authoritative person, who was most anxious to know all about him and to make certain he was sent to the right pigeon-hole. It seems that those in authority had known about them all along, but had to collect up a certain number of recruits before they could begin to do anything with them.

THE ROBIN

Who killed Cock Robin? – The sparrow admitted it, so that was all right.

That question being disposed of, there was endless discussion about a funeral. Where should it take place? What form should it take? Who should have what function? Flowers. Music. A fine coffin. Reverence. Last rest.

Cock Robin found it all highly amusing. It sounded as though they were burying him, rather than so much rotting meat, a carcase he had once used but abandoned with the impact of the sparrow's arrow.

THE ROCKBIRD

That loneliness is demoralizing has always been recognized by those who are interested in the subjection of their fellows. The only counter, obviously enough, is an inner resource capable of erecting an invincible resistance. Perhaps there are several ways of achieving this. The one used for thousands of years by religious martyrs of all persuasions is what they would doubtless think of as an intimate relationship with God. (Those who are disposed to do so may choose to call this auto-suggestion. It doesn't really matter.) If it is possible for God to be a reality for one, then logically there can be no such thing as solitary confinement.

THE
ROOK

In a certain part of the countryside, just hidden from the road, there is a sort of water meadow with a fold in the middle, which is the source of our stream. – Although less than half a mile away across the fields from our mill-race here, it is four or five miles by the course of the stream. On one side the meadow climbs fairly sharply to a bluff, which is the highest point of this particular portion of the hills. Along the crest of the bluff is a line of tall elm trees.

In winter (which it was at the time I speak of: there was thin snow on the hills, and the gathering stream was trimmed with fragile ice), in winter when the trees were bare the rooks' nests could be seen. It was – still is – surely one of the biggest rookeries in these parts.

There was at that time a gang of young rooks among the residents, who were perpetually making a nuisance of themselves. Whether it was vice, malice, devilment, boredom, or just high spirits, who should say? They would circle about endlessly, swooping suddenly on anyone unsuspecting, teasing or making mock attacks on their more peaceable neighbours, and shouting and screaming all the time. It was difficult to know how to deal with this menace. Some said punish them severely, others said be specially kind to them; some said give them something to do, others said ignore them. The argument went on so endlessly that some other urgent problem had always come up before a solution had been in sight. So nothing was ever done, and the young rooks went on as they had always done.

One bitterly cold January morning, after an hour or two of their usual fun, the gang members and hangers-on returned to their own nests. One of the noisiest (if not of the most prominent in other respects) was feeling rather depressed; he was dissatisfied with himself. This was because he knew that by all considerations he should have been above such raucous and unconstructive behaviour. The more he thought about it the more disgusted he was with himself. How could he – educated, intelligent, decently brought up, etc., etc. – how could he bring himself to join in such goings on?

The gang was going to call for him in the afternoon. He resolved not to go with them. They could beg him, threaten him, mock him; he would tell them he had finished with that kind of life. What a pity, he thought, that he had no other friends; then he could have slipped away and gone with them, and the gang would hardly have bothered to search for him. Well, he could slip away on his own. No, that would look like sulking. Besides, where could he go? What could he do? What would he say when he met one of the gang? The only way was to tell them exactly what was what when they came.

He could hear them coming. His heart thudded alarmingly. They arrived and circled in front of him, screeching and braying. What would he do? He opened his mouth. And shut it again. What are you waiting for? He couldn't be alone. Will you come on? He joined them. His cackle was the loudest of all.

THE RUBYTHROAT

'... the shape of loneliness, greenly
irridescent, whitely indefinite, seemed
to rise from the garden ...'
(*Other Voices, Other Rooms*)

In the sultry afternoon the garden shimmered. But otherwise it was lifeless; one bird alone hovered uncertainly. It was an open garden, having nothing to conceal, no secretive life; when creatures were there they were seen to be there and the place woke up. The bird wondered why no one else was about.

Beyond the wall was a jungly piece of waste ground, luxuriant with nettles and poisonous plants of every description, decaying richly. All manner of evil seemed to be promised by this tract; the air low above it, cloying and enticing, was heavy and dank and palpably unhealthy. And it gave the impression of concealing much. The small bird flew very high over it, but after a while, with curiosity and irresolution, slowed and descended a little. Could that be where his companions had gone?

THE
SANDPIPER

There is a well-known story about a group of people belonging to various religious orders who were saying the office together – when the lights went out. The Benedictines went on as though nothing had happened. The Franciscans immediately began to pray for light. The Dominicans started a discussion on the theology of light. The Jesuits went and mended the fuse.

The story is apocryphal of course. But, besides catching the character of these four orders rather nicely, it also illustrates the four basic approaches to religion and to life.

The Benedictine reaction is the philosophical approach, a calm acceptance of what comes – no excitement, no fuss, no recrimination. Critics have called it a fatalistic approach.

The Franciscan reaction is the pious approach (and that's not meant in a derogatory sense), the response when something goes wrong of promptly falling on one's knees and asking God to do something about it.

The Dominican reaction obviously is the intellectual approach, the desire to work things out and understand them.

And the Jesuit reaction is the pragmatic approach, concerned not so much with what in theory ought to be done as with what in practice will actually work.

There is no suggestion that any one of these approaches is better than the others. They're all equally valid, and which one any individual is most drawn to will depend on his own temperament.

But it would surely be wrong to develop exclusively one type of response, and it would certainly be dangerous to carry any of them to extremes. An over-indulged passivity, a piety which neglects action, an intellectualism which *replaces* faith, an activism which tends to leave no room for the Holy Spirit – all these are clearly insufficient. We need a balanced approach. We need to trust, we need to pray, we need to think, and we need to act. All these things are part of the Christian response.

So much for that. But perhaps it may be relevant to apply these approaches also to the problem of loneliness. For, amongst the lonely, there must be those who accept loneliness, those who pray about it, those who talk about it, and those who try to do something about it. And, indeed, those who do all four things.

THE
SAPSUCKER

The people of the valley had been fruit-farming for generations, but they had never seen a sapsucker, for the species had not at that time moved so far west. When the first sapsucker arrived one spring they were rather pleased, for he was a friendly creature, and pretty to watch as he flashed about the orchards. He remained the only bird of his kind there, and so became rather a pet, and the workers would give him a cheerful greeting each morning.

But it happened that that year was a bad one for the farmers; the fruits were few and small and not full of flavour. The farmers and their workers looked for a cause, and the first thing they noticed was that the trees had holes in the bark, which the sapsucker had made in order to get at the juices underneath. Concluding therefore that it was the sapsucker who had occasioned the poor fruit, they turned on him and threw stones whenever they saw him, so that before long he left the valley. He was bewildered at this change of attitude, and hurt by it, and wondered what cause he had given to be hounded away.

Beware experience. You can experience many a happening, but you can never experience all the occurrences of any one kind of happening. The people of the valley now know from experience that sapsuckers are a menace to fruit. But they are wrong. The holes the sapsuckers make, and the loss of the juices they extract, don't harm the trees or the fruit in the least. And since sapsuckers also feed on borers and other insects who really harm the trees and the fruit, they are in fact beneficial.

THE
SEAGULL

High on the headland you wanded
As we fled over the phantom waves
Away away
The wind in your hair
Made willowing storms
Of your treesoft tresses and wept
Pale foaming tears of blue
Across the sobbing bay
Which enchanted us wailing
Away.

High on the headland you towered
Than the towering headland
Higher higher
Your yodelling hair
Brought by the arching
Seaswept breeze
Over the water to us

Who fled who fled
Unwanting unwitting
Over the sea
But not till oblivious voyage's end
Out of the sight of you.

THE
SECRETARY BIRD

Rye-voiced the bosses seemed
Berhinestoned-wived
At bridge the afternoon themselves all golfed
Maternity-shirted mock-Hawaiian
And burned-skinned from the jetted beach.

(Jaundice and venom of the lonely eye).

Soft-eyed by music hard in the light of day
Hopping in red-rimmed circles round the intercom
As though to intrigue for a directorate of Heaven.

If the sun is but their reflection
And the swinging moon a fly-trap of Venus,
That's Life, boy.

THE SHAG

She was a scruffy old thing. Her person she contrived to keep comparatively clean, but her nest was filthy and lice-ridden. If you met her out and about she would stop and chat gaily for hours; but if you visited her at home she would regard you with suspicion, so that those who tried to take an interest in her were put off and left her alone. This was thoroughly understandable but a great pity, since a bit of company was probably all the incentive she needed. She had retained sufficient of her self-respect to be ashamed of her squalor, but not enough to do anything about it.

THE SHEARWATER

I'm told that we shearwaters are the greatest travellers of all. Certainly we 'get around', as they say. One thing about travelling is that you meet all sorts of people. On one trip I saw a great deal of a particular couple who've always stuck in my mind. They were on their way to a new country, where the husband hoped to live out of contact with other people as far as possible.

He and I were agreed on one thing; we both hated herds. But from there we went in opposite directions. If I think of people in the abstract, especially of 'the people', I don't like people. But individually, when I get to know them, I always do like people; there are very few indeed who are wholly unlikeable. But he extended his dislike of people in general to people in particular. He had no use for his fellow men, and spoke slightingly of everyone who came in view. On the other hand this didn't prevent him from being devoted to the idea of 'the people'. He would endlessly expound left-wing politics, in terms of the clichés of a bygone age.

His feelings and ideas were entirely matters of principle; he told us constantly what he did or didn't do as a matter of principle. Myself, I'm not much interested in principles, only in realities; the one thing I really loathe is party lines and doctrinaire opinions.

He was naturally opposed to religion and spent considerable time and words in demolishing it to his satisfaction, though his knowledge of it being rudimentary, and the notions he struck at being childlike and primitive and unreal, one couldn't take it very seriously. He said he had no need of religion, and that he had grown out of God. He didn't notice that he had made a religion of his opinions and a god of himself.

His wife loyally shared his views. But it was a lonely life for her at the best of times, and one felt very sorry for her going out to live alone with him in the wilderness (though I doubt if she would have appreciated anyone's sympathy). His attitude was born of loneliness, but so fiercely did he cling to it that he was not lonely with it. For her, however, this attitude could hardly fail to be a cause of loneliness.

But on those occasions when he could be got to talk of something other than himself, and when he wasn't nervous and excited, he was kind and gentle and gay. One felt that if only one could get near enough to offer real companionship he was capable of becoming a different person.

THE SKUA

The skua is one of the most sea-going of birds, very experienced in the ways of all seafarers, and he had this to say about sea captains:

'The captain of a ship bears a degree of responsibility far beyond anything in any comparable shore job, and he bears it in an aloneness quite unknown to those even in the highest office ashore. It may be that he can confide in and ask the advice of his senior officers over some of his problems, and it may be that he can't. A ship doesn't have a committee, or a vestry, or a synod, or a board of directors, or governors, or managers, or a council, or a cabinet, or whatever name such a mechanism for collective responsibility may be given. Executive decisions are the captain's. And towards the crew, he must if necessary be both father and mother, and wise uncle: both jury and judge, and probation officer: a confessor sometimes, an adviser often: a physician sometimes, a psychologist all the time. And always he must comport himself as a man to be respected but not feared, a man in whom to have unbounded confidence. A good master mariner must therefore be a man of extraordinary gifts – a man, that is, whom neither power nor loneliness will corrupt.'

THE
SMEW

One afternoon the smew (aged at that time three or four) and his nanny went for a walk in the fields nearby. One of these fields was, for some reason, surrounded by a high wall with a single opening. The smew was in this field when he suddenly noticed that his nanny wasn't there. He had never been alone before, except at night in his own bed, and panic seized him. The gap in the wall seemed to have vanished, and he was convinced he was on his own in an entirely inescapable enclosure. He flew round the field time and again (so it seemed) with an utter terror; here he was, separated from all other creatures by that insurmountable wall. In reality of course the opening was there, and as soon as he came to it he found it, and there was the nanny sitting on the bank beside it.

THE
SNIPE

At one time I taught in a school for the sons of gentlesnipe. We got a variety of pupils there. One I remember in particular. He was healthy enough physically, a strapping young bird. But psychologically he was rather a mess. He did the most stupid things – never in fact did anything right. And he couldn't open his mouth without saying something annoying and ridiculous. He was a constant irritation to the staff and the other pupils alike. Consequently of course he had a pretty thin time of it.

Steinbeck has noted that 'Once a boy has suffered rejection, he will find rejection even where it does not exist – or, worse, will draw it forth from people simply by expecting it'. Well, this young snipe was one like that.

But then, after he'd been there a good few months we had an unusually severe frost, and the big pond froze over and became a playground. Lo and behold! our useless and despised member was the star performer on ice. From then on he was accepted as a reasonable bird after all, and he immediately began to do things right and to speak sensibly.

It seems there is a need to prove to oneself that one is capable of something or other before one can begin to feel acceptable, and that one has to feel acceptable before one can let oneself be acceptable. Perhaps creatures older than this snipe might do it by an act of sex. In the schoolboy world it usually has to be something athletic.

THE SOLDIERBIRD

Out of Dindymus heavily laden
Like troop trains bound for a distant front
Drifting through the suburbs
One heard the sad slow drawing-room piano waltzes.

Long-skirted maidens all alone
Gazed blankly into the cavernous windows
Of the empty shops,
As though awaiting some golden Lethe
That would presently flow out of them
As blood and love pour from the wounded heart.

The yellowing early leaves were falling
Almost purposefully from the trees
And songs of strident melancholy
Came thinly from the cafés.
– 'Wer weiss ob wir uns wiedersehen
Am schönen Strand der Spree'.

THE SPARROW

I was caught by the birdseller and taken to market, where I was bought by a boy, I and my companion. There was a fellow standing by watching. He turned to a friend and said:

'Look at that. Two sparrows are sold for a penny. Yet even a bird of such small account shall not die without our father in heaven knowing about it.'

My companion died very soon afterwards. I often wonder if this father in heaven does know about it. And if he knows what will happen to me.

THE SPARROWHAWK

The granite setts of Spandau's broad streets, damply covered by a little snow, echoed the arrival of the new guard. It was the end of a midwinter afternoon, and the discouraged sun was departing. From the cavalry barracks a few blocks away came the sound of Retreat.

High up on the walls of the citadel the sparrowhawk sighed. It wasn't his confinement that troubled him. It was the fact that he alone was left, still alive after all these years, to ponder the heady time of power and effort, the unique comradeship of that brilliant though inevitably tragic epoch.

THE SQUACCO

If you were to visit our squacco geriatrics' hospital you would find all sorts of interesting characters there. Some are there voluntarily, to spare their families or friends as they get less capable; some are there against their will because their families can't cope; some are there because they need full-time medical care.

Many of them are incontinent. Some because they're not physically capable of being anything else, some because they're too shy to ask and so make extra work for the nurse (though to their shame and agony they are really well aware that in the event it makes much more), and some out of pure devilment.

Most of them live for the visiting hours. The majority have families in the vicinity, and those are pretty good at visiting them.

And of course being the sort of locality it is there are plenty of professional and voluntary visitors. Some of those who don't have families claim they don't wish to be visited. Others genuinely prefer not to be, because it disturbs their reading or their thoughts; but as the years pass and these occupations pall they're glad enough if anyone stops.

A lot depends on the relationship between the old people and the nurse. Often there is a degree of mutual fear, especially among those who are new. Some patients are difficult, through pain or awkwardness or ill-nature – there are those who take the view that since nurses are paid to look after them it's up to the patients to ensure that whoever pays them gets his money's worth. The occasional nurse reacts badly to this and becomes hard, but she's very much an exception.

Some of the patients never move, but just lie there vacantly, while others are extremely lively – mentally at least, and occasionally physically so as well. There is one who is quite young but with an extremely active and happy mind, but multiple sclerosis has condemned her. Another cheerful soul has, through paralysis, been there twenty-two years, since she was quite a young girl. There is a toothless old rip who, whenever a nurse bends over the bed to tuck him in, pulls her on top of him. Another gets a tremendous kick out of endless quarrels about which television channel they should watch. Another will (only if invited) talk entertainingly for hours of his boyhood seventy years ago. By and large those who still have life in them are as delightful a collection of old birds as you'll find.

THE STORK

Storks are birds with a great sense of rectitude, despite their ruthlessly pragmatic approach to their perennial problem. (You must know that a pair of storks, since they can only support two young on the long migration, will always heave the third one out of the nest).

Once I heard two storks discussing the morality of this practice. The first said: 'Dandolo the Doge of Venice and the German knight Werner von Borland were on their way to the Fourth Crusade. The German thought better of it and went home with all his followers, which the Venetian leaders felt was a catastrophe. But Dandolo told them of what we have to do, and they were reassured.'

The second replied: 'That is irrelevant. The Venetians were only making the best of a bad job. And von Borland had nothing to suffer. You've heard of Merry and Bright, the comedy team? They were doing very nicely in a second-rate sort of way, when Merry received an excellent offer for long-term star billing provided he dropped Bright. He accepted.'

The first argued: 'That is equally irrelevant. Merry sacrificed Bright to his own personal vanity. That is a different matter from jeopardising the safety of the greater number.'

'But', rejoined the second, 'whether many or few gained from it doesn't alter the amount of suffering inflicted on the one who loses.'

Here the discussion petered out. After all, they were only birds.

THE
SUNBITTERN

He was rather a nondescript individual, shabby, not good-looking, and extremely diffident; so diffident in fact that the awkwardness of his manner often gave the impression that he was rude. This in turn, since he was sensitive and aware that he put people off, made him even more nervous of them, and he tended to have no more contact than was necessary with his fellows. – Not that he didn't want the contact; he just couldn't face the possible rebuffs.

To make matters worse he was out of work at the moment. He had been taken on as a clerk on a temporary basis but had hoped it would become permanent; unfortunately it didn't. There was something vaguely indecent about being without work, he couldn't help feeling. He dreaded having to go the rounds looking for a new job, but there was nothing else for it. This apprehension, on the top of his perpetual loneliness and shyness, made life a bit of a nightmare just at present.

He wanted of course to find a wife like everybody else, but had completely despaired of ever doing so. One good friend had suggested he should go to dances, where one could meet people of all sorts, even such a quiet and understanding female as he would need. He knew he could never bring himself to do that, but even though he had no intention of taking it up the suggestion had remained with him. Now, when he was at bottom, a nothing-matters mood took hold of him, and as he couldn't in any case stand the loneliness of his room he resolved to go to a dance; he had seen one advertised earlier in the day.

As he entered the hall his usual fear of people returned and he almost went out again. But the worry that he would make an even bigger fool of himself by doing that than by staying prevented him. He hadn't really intended actually to dance, simply to come and see if he could meet anyone. But when, having looked round and seen a gentle-looking girl sitting by herself, he went up to her, the only thing he could think of to say was to ask her to dance.

It was a waltz, an undistinguished modern waltz. The girl danced rather mechanically and she was hardly beautiful, but it was the first time he had ever held one, and in the pride of this achievement nothing else mattered. Fortunately she didn't seem to expect any conversation, which was a relief. Round and round the room they went, a commonplace couple doing a commonplace dance in a politely commonplace manner.

But the time changed (was that real or imaginary?), and became an Edwardian waltz, elegant, sentimental, and wistful – gay, that is, but as though with the warning of a sadness to come. The girl smiled, and became more animated, though she still didn't talk. Suddenly he knew the meaning of companionship. He gripped her, and did his best to make his movements match the music in grace. A new dread took hold of him, a dread that the music would stop, because it seemed to him that that would be the end, and he would return to loneliness, a loneliness which would be all the worse after this glimpse of something different.

Then the music changed again, it seemed. This time it was a Viennese waltz, played with evocativeness and a satiny verve that swept them up into an ecstasy of decorous abandon. The girl had now completely accepted him; her head was on his breast, her movements one with his effortlessly and gladly. A new thought came to him; a bigger fear took hold of him. This, he thought, was the reality, and the life he knew the dream. He knew then that once the music stopped the reality would be gone and nightmare would return for evermore.

Once more the music changed. Now it was one of those Russian concert waltzes. So fast there was no time to think where one was putting one's feet, only to concentrate on moving them to keep up with the rhythm. Feverishly they danced, much faster than they could have run. Faces raced past them, round and round, up and down, like the grinning horses of a roundabout that's gone wildly out of control. Faster. Faster still. Madly they went. The faces blurred into one, a crazy ribbon of paleness jagging across the colours like a crooked stripe on a child's top. No longer conscious of anything but the insistence of the pace they clung to each other and whirled.

THE
SUPERB BIRD
OF PARADISE

In human terms loneliness is an insufficiency of human relationships. In theological terms perhaps (I don't know) it's true to say that loneliness is the result of the lack of a (or at least an imperfect) relationship with God. The goal of a Christian (presumably of any theist) is knowledge of God. The better we get to know God the more we are (or should be) able to adjust our lives in such a way that we don't become lonely – and also see to it that others don't. And yet according to the Creation narrative it seems that man's fall was occasioned by his seeking for knowledge. But in fact that knowledge which, we are told, man got into trouble over was not knowledge of God but knowledge of things which only God was supposed to be allowed to know about.

In seeking to understand the Creation story it is important to be able to distinguish between its fundamental truth and the fundamental mythology in which it is set. Poetically and theologically this narrative is true; this is how things are between God and us. Historically and scientifically we know very well it's not true; since the first two chapters of Genesis give contradictory accounts it would be hard to believe anyway.

In the third chapter we meet the serpent. There are two aspects of this serpent, the folk-loric aspect and the symbolic aspect. The first is shown in the explanation given of how the eternal relationship between man and snake came to be defined. This reminds one very much of Kipling's story 'The Cat that Walked by Itself', in which an explanation is given of how the relationship between man and cat came to be defined. (Incidentally it mustn't be supposed that we can only learn about God from books intended to be religious. I think there's a lot of theology in the *Just So Stories*, as in any work which is deeply observant of life.)

As to the symbolism of the serpent, obviously here it is chiefly intended as a symbol of evil. But it has been used for other purposes. Traditionally it's a symbol of wisdom; Matthew quotes

Jesus as using the simile 'wise as serpents' when sending out the apostles, and Nietzsche uses it in the same sense. It has meant healing – look at a caduceus, and remember Moses' totem in the Book of Numbers. And from its ability to acquire a new skin it was used in ancient times as a symbol of mysterious knowledge.

It would appear that the author of this passage in Genesis was aware of these traditions, for the serpent offers man secret knowledge, properly belonging to God alone. In the writer's understanding knowledge, wisdom, and healing, though good, belong to God, and when usurped by man become (at least potentially) evil. Our understanding of God has developed a good deal since those days, and our understanding of our relationship with him is that these things are good and remain good so long as we use them for his purposes. In other words we believe that the maximum good of the world is an end and that we have a mandate to use all means which have been or may be revealed to us to that end.

Now if for a moment we were to take the characters of the narrative as actual people, we could well believe that Adam and Eve felt for some reason neglected by God and made friends with the serpent out of loneliness (and hence, perhaps, spite). And on the other hand (though it was clearly not intended to mean any such thing) we could take the expulsion from Eden as saying: 'If man thinks he can do without God, let him try'. Theologically speaking, the existence of *real* loneliness dates from that moment.

THE SWALLOW

A lot of swallows used to live in our settlement, all exiles from their own countries, Some had been driven out by international agreements, some by new and terrible governments; some had found their territories taken over by other species (mostly on spurious historical grounds – either that the predecessor government had been their suzerain or that the land had once been taken from them). There were many reasons for exile, but it was always involuntary.

They would congregate in melancholy little groups and endlessly discuss their return, which they were passionately hopeful of while at the same time knowing it would never happen. Though some of us mocked at it, this was a real and consuming sadness to them.

THE SWAN

The swan woke early. That was because of the cold; for some time before he was properly awake he had been aware of a feeling of chill creeping round his underparts and gradually penetrating his body. The nest he had built for himself was a poor affair, scarcely big enough for his bulk and certainly not strong enough for his weight. He had not taken the trouble to collect sufficient materials, nor of the right sort, and had hardly bothered at all about building them together properly. He was so tired these days; everything was so much effort, and there seemed no point in troubling. He was old, very old, and lonely; only a remnant of self-respect was left, which still drove him to keep his feathers white, though there was no one else on this mountain lake to see him, and to search intermittently for food. Now the weight of his body was forcing the ill-constructed nest apart till it let him into the icy water.

The sky was a sheet of indigo stretched taut and low over the lake; only to the east a thin pallid line told of the advent of morning. There was no breeze at all; the chill was in the shallow layer of autumn mist that hung an inch or two above the surface of the water. There was no sign of any other living creature, no motion anywhere. The sedges were still, crests drooping, like grasses growing on the grave of Hope. It was as though the world had ended and this corner of it been forgotten.

The swan, without moving his body, stretched his cramped feet a little and tried to blow out his feathers in an effort to keep away the cold. Wearily he opened his eyes. He was surprised to see that his little island of decaying vegetation was no longer fast among the sedge but was with infinite slowness drifting out into open water. Now this sort of thing was liable to happen when, for instance, the water level changed – especially with a badly made nest such as his, and normally there was nothing to be done but let the old nest float away and oneself return to shore and start afresh. Instinctively the swan started to withdraw himself from the raft, but he was at once convinced that he had neither the energy at that moment to regain the shallows nor the heart to start again. He decided to stay with his nest and let it carry him wherever it was going, until it disintegrated or grounded in the rushes in another corner of the lake.

Somehow this involuntary launching out towards an unknown destination put him in mind of his birth, which he could not of course remember. He was still moving very very slowly, just as life seems to at the beginning. What would he come to? What had he come to? Had he thought of these things then? Had it mattered? Did it matter? He abandoned all thought of the future and settled his mind into that most bittersweet of presents, the past. It did not matter that the past he was groping for was one he could not have recalled; he knew that it was good and full of promise. He was no longer cold. His body was numb now, and felt neither the chill of the water nor the clammy caress of the water-weed. And so, without hope and without fear, he moved almost imperceptibly across the lake.

After a while he opened his eyes again. It was lighter now, and he could see that he was being drawn to where the lake narrowed into the beginning of the little stream which was its outlet. There were willows along the bank of the stream, which with their pollarded heads in the halflight looked like a row of still and silent women that the swirls of mist around their trunks turned into ballerinas. The sheep had not been in this part of the mountains lately, so the grass was long, and wisps of it hung across the water or floated on the surface like the hair of a hundred uncelebrated Ophelias. The flow of the stream was not fast here anyway, and the grass catching at the stalks and leaves of his remnant of nest slowed the swan's progress still further, so that it seemed to take an age to go from tree to tree. He counted them as he passed, each one seeming the ghost of a life's year, some straight and strong and others twisted and thin, and one or two almost falling across the brook.

It was on just such a stream as this, with willows but without the long grass, that he had first gone swimming with his parents. The sun had been shining – it seemed the sun always shone in those days. The stream was shallow with a stony bed; the surface broke into diamond ripples which caught the sunlight and made a pattern on the bed like frosted wire-netting. Kingcups grew in it, and watercress, and on the banks forget-me-nots, and where it turned and widened into little pools tadpoles moved busily in indeterminate directions. Calves came shyly to the water's edge and sometimes started nervously at seeing their own reflections stare seriously back. As the summer wore on more and more flowers came out on the bank, and the level of the water fell till there was scarcely enough to turn the wheel of the sawmill in the valley – the mill whence came the sweet smell of fresh moist sawdust and the drowsy drone of the saw on hot afternoons. Then came the autumn rains. No, the sun had not shone always after all; that was only an illusion of the golden age. The swan remembered following his parents along the stream while the drops of rain ran down the leaves of the lindens and whitebeams that bordered it at one point, and off them, leaping through the air to disappear with a hollow sound into a neat circle of water. It filled him with a sadness he could never quite account for, a sense of a vanished youngness that was not his own, an ineffably touching secret which always just

149

eluded him. After the rains the stream would soon regain its level, and then become deeper and deeper until it overflowed its banks and covered the meadows, and one had the unaccustomed excitement of swimming up sunken lanes between brambles and hazel bushes, and sometimes almost into farmyards. If the hard frost came before the floods had subsided there were acres of ice to walk across before food could be found, and every twig was coated in ice like a delicate glass toy, so that all seemed brittle and one walked cautiously lest it should break. It seemed an age after the ice and snow had gone and it was just cold and dull until things happened again, but eventually tiny rolls of the palest green appeared on the branches and the flowers came out – first snowdrops, then violets, primroses, daffodils, and celandines – and then suddenly one day lambs would be carolling in the meadows and all was bright again. Life in his childhood had been wonderful – the swan realized this when he was still very young. But it seemed so impossible to explain; even others who had been alive at the time seemed quite unable to grasp how magically different everything was in those days, how indefinably but singingly perfect.

The upland meadows had been passed now, and the stream was picking its way along a brackeny hillside. The sun hovered redly. The trees, hawthorns mostly, hung back as though afraid of some enchantment. The bracken naturally was brown, but it gave the impression of having died not recently but many summers past. It was a time of softly lingering decay.

It had been this time of year when the swan was first without his parents, and from then on the period after Michaelmas seemed to him always the most poignant. In autumn he had learned to play with others of his own age on a chain of willowed and islanded ponds, taking rough knocks from the boisterous games and infinitely rougher mental knocks from the careless intolerance of his fellows. For the first time he discovered that life was not perfect, that often squalor lay, like an ancient leper in a velvet dress, behind a fair façade. On one of the streams they used there was a sudden turn to the right and the water fell vertically ten or twelve feet into a rocky dell thick with wild garlic and anemones; but the dell was strewn with bottomless pots and the rusty springs of what had been a bed. In winter, though, sometimes the waterfall froze solid, and then all was lovely, for snow covered the ailing metal and the water as it froze collected at the sides of the fall, making gradually two shining pillars which framed the entrance to a little cave, normally hidden by the water, in which grew plants found nowhere else. And the trickle of water which took the stream's overflow round the waterfall down a steep but not vertical slope froze too, making a slippery chute which the young swans delighted in sliding down, forgetting for the moment feuds and unhappinesses. Those days were not unhappy on the whole, but they bred in the swan his apartness, his sense of being unable to support for long the presence of others because of a great gulf in understanding that separated them from him, his acceptance of the need to be alone in spite of an often aching loneliness. In that particular summer of his boyhood which followed the first sad autumn and the slightly less strange winter he swam alone for hours up narrow streams, watching the kingfisher darting along the water or the heron silent and motionless on a branch too small for him.

He was reminded of the heron by the sight of one rising before him from the water with a fish held crosswise in his beak. The stream turned here to begin its plunge down the side of the mountains, and the speed of its flow increased at once. All trace of the nest had vanished now; the swan was riding naked in the water, eyes closed, no muscle moving, just drifting as the current took him, sometimes swung sideways or rocked over on one flank like a rubber toy in a bath. The stream began to move even faster, careering down the hillside like a schoolboy late for callover, and the swan abandoned himself to the motion he could do nothing to prevent, feeling the sick terror of one on a fairground amusement. As he was swept along on the torrent thoughts of his turbulent adolescence blew in and out of his mind as leaves flow in and out of an unglazed tower on a day of November gales – little regretful memories of the thousand petty meannesses and stupidities that had spoiled his behaviour and so his relations with others in those days and had returned in odd moments of leisure later on to torment him. As the stream twisted and turned and bumped him physically along its mad descent, so these rapid recollections beset his slowing brain, and he was in a state of breathlessness and incoherence when the stream took a final dive under a thicket of elm bushes into the valley river and threw him right across it into a pool concaved out of the further bank.

For a long time he sat on the water dazedly beside an elder root. The main current flowed outside this cove and the pull within was very slight and, such as it was, counteracted where he was by the root. Eventually he opened his eyes to find a thinly shining sun and the surface of the water in the little bay herringboned by a breeze. By now he was too weak to move at all, but very gradually the drag of the river was working him down the side of the root till soon he was at the end of it, and then he floated free and quickly drifted into the mainstream of the river. He was quite without the ability to influence his movements, and equally without the will, but followed passively the caprice of the current as it drew him, quite slowly here, along. Both banks were wooded, not densely but with young birches; there would be bluebells at another season. The sun was shining more strongly and, since the trees were leafless, fell often on the water. The heart of the swan was more at rest than hitherto that morning.

One sunny morning years before he had set out young but fully grown to seek not his fortune but the world. He was free; there was nothing to keep him in any one place; he could do what he cared to and wander where he would. To know this and to be fit and eager and to float along briskly on a warm summer's morning was the most joyous thing imaginable. And he had gone on enjoying it for some years, exploring brooks and rivers broad and narrow and fast and slow, and lakes lonely or frequented, wild dark tarns on rocky hills, muddy estuaries, busy harbours, park ponds, filthy back-street warehouse-bordered canals, carefully tended water-gardens, moorland swamps and dewponds and marshland rhines, and salt lagoons behind the duny shore. He had flown across the sea more than once, not hurrying but with a calm and splendid beat, almost as graceful in flight as on the water. Finally he had come back to where he had started from, not satisfied, but still with a restless longing to find he did not know what.

The river had left the wood now and was flowing, still smoothly, between low thick bushes on the right and deserted pastures on the left. Soon it brought the swan to a place he recognized. There was a low stone bridge which carried a byroad with one bound over the river, and just before it was a sudden widening, out of which led a shallow slope that the cattle came down to drink. For some reason the fish liked this shallow pool, and they swam so thickly there one could not avoid touching them. Once a dead branch shaped curiously like a set of bagpipes had lain at the top of the slope, till a little boy had found it and marched all an afternoon up and down the field playing the battle music of his fathers until the grey evening came and he was fetched home to tea. The reason the swan recognized this place so unfailingly was that it had been here he had met his mate.

One evening in summer he had come sailing down the river prepared to spend the night somewhere at hand and early next morning fly across country to new waters. As he came round the curve he saw a young shy pen emerging from the arch of the bridge, her eyes scanning diffidently yet eagerly the scene revealed to her in the light of the setting sun after her dark passage through the tunnel under the bridge. She caught sight of him, and seemed pleased to find a probable friend. She too, he soon found, was a seeker, a lone journeyer, but not with the same biting restlessness that drove him always on. Together they found and ate their evening food, and side by side they settled into two white huddles on the bank for the night.

The next day they had swum slowly the stretch of water the swan was drifting down now, over the pebbly ford where the white horse crossed, past the end of the orchard where the apples then young and sharp on the bough now rolled rotten into the water. From time to time they twined their necks together, or toyed wantonly with drops of water. Once he had made a garland for her from the honeysuckle trailing in the water, which filled her feathers with a humming fragrance. All day they paddled playfully downstream, not noticing how little distance they covered, and certainly not caring, until it was evening again and they came to an almost landlocked inlet beneath a low cliff crowned with a wood and firs, and here they decided to live for a while.

The swan's eyesight was failing, and he peered hard as he passed the spot where he knew the inlet was. The shape of it had changed considerably in the intervening years; the spit of sand which used to cut it off almost completely from the river had been washed away, and the cliff behind had crumbled and filled in the back part of the pool, so that it was now crabbed and ugly in shape like the mouth of a petulant child. This is the way of life, he knew, for things cannot be kept indefinitely as they are; nor can they be returned to with any expectation of finding them the same. All things must change: but at a certain speed – for if the fates are rushed the rusher's work is soon undone again, as a hole dug in the beach is filled in by the succeeding tide. Making an effort to move

for the first time that day the swan tried to turn his neck for a last
look at the scene of so much happiness as he was carried into the
gorge below, a narrow rocky defile which deepened and confined
the river as his life had been deepened and confined by his mating.
His restlessness, though not entirely banished, had been largely
assuaged by it. He no longer had the irresistible urge to wander,
but sometimes even yet his spirit craved – something, he still could
not tell what. On this day in his feebleness, when little will was left
to him but only the power of burning recollection, he smiled
within himself to think of it as he was born along on the strong and
silent current through the gorge.

Very soon it widened, and the river widened with it and grew
shallow, though the pace did not change. The cliffs became lower
and untidier, and broken lumps of boulder lay in the water. The
swan was hurtled along, bumping from rock to rock and scraping
over jagged points of stone on the river bed, almost drowned by
the spray thrown in his face, his feet caught in twigs of great
branches lying among the boulders. He had not been so scratched
and bruised since his fight with the dog. This had happened on a
towpath beside a navigable stretch of a large river; the towpath in
fact separated the river from a flooded swamp that ran alongside it,
and here in the reeds, screened from the towpath by a clump of
bushed, he had built with infinite love and patience a strong and
comfortable nest for his mate's first confinement. Shortly after the
birth a dog, a large terrier, had come along the tow path and started
nosing his way into the bushes. The swan, who had been idling
complacently on the water, stalked up the bank, raised himself
erect as tall as he could make himself, and spread his wings. The
dog began to retire at once, and then suddenly changed his mind
and sprang at the swan't throat. For a very few seconds there was a
confusion of noise and movement, and then all at once the dog was
tearing battered and bleeding down the towpath and the swan,
equally battered and bleeding, remained panting by the nest.

The rapids past, the swan was swept round a last bend of
majestic radius and there before him was the great river which the
small one joined at an angle. On the narrow point of land between
the two a wild goose stood without moving, its beak stretched
towards the sky. Beyond the great river, far away on the hillside,
lay a small town; the whole landscape seemed to belong to the
realm of the backgrounds of great pictures. The momentum of the
small river carried the swan into midstream of the larger one, and

seen from the bank he must have appeared the picture of grace and nobility a swan should be as the river carried him with it in its progress, the imperturbable progress of a great waterway that never dries up or plays similar tricks but is always confident of its power and importance, unrushed, unlistening, complacent, irresistible, carrying the débris of a continent to dump it in the sea. Little more than débris the swan felt himself to be, for he knew now what awaited him. Powerless to order anything about his fate, he would be carried out to sea till the last drop of fresh water was lost in the salt, and there his scarcely living flesh would be at the mercy of sharks and the ravenous seabirds.

The sun was now a little past its zenith – or rather not the sun but the place where its presence was indicated by the paler hole in a lias sky. The swan was drifting down towards a bridge – several bridges – leading into the city on the right bank. Mourning willows of considerable antiquity and size hung over the inshore water, and behind them rose tiers of grey buildings culminating in the tower of a cathedral. The swan and his mate had lived in a city for some time when their young were small. It had been pleasant on fine afternoons to swim sedately beside the bank while the people admired them and sometimes threw them cakes and an occasional young poet tried desperately to squeeze them into an adequate piece of verse. He had been in his prime then, a magnificent bird, acknowledged by all as the pride of the river. He thought of this a little wistfully as he passed under the last bridge out into the country again.

When the young swans had grown up and departed he and his mate had moved to a backwater, one much like one of those he began to pass soon after leaving the city. So overhung with trees were they as to be almost tunnels; houseboats for gentle misanthropists were moored there, close against the shore in thick bushes, without a sign of life; only the clouds of midges brought the afternoon a decadent activity. This time in the backwater had been but an interlude, a period of readjustment, that had not lasted long, and the swans had soon passed on to other scenes as he was carried now into a gradually flattening area of pastures.

Smooth and tranquil the later years of their life together had been. Harmony was the standard of their lives, and all they touched became harmonious. They chose still waters, and travelled slowly if at all. The peace which passes understanding was upon them. And then one evening in a forsaken creek not far from the coast drained by drought and the ebb tide till the living water was only a trickle across acres of reeking mud, his mate was taken ill. The sky had suddenly cast over and then cracked, and the wind drove stinging lictors' rods of rain which crushed the reeds and made punch holes in the mud and then passed out to sea. All that night the swan watched fearfully beside his mate; but when the early light crept sniggering up the creek, she died.

For months the swan had dreaded to be alone and always gone where friends and life were, attaching his pale company to theirs like a preoccupied ghost. But in the end he had flown off to the mountains to the wildest place he knew to be alone and wait. He had lived on the mountain lake a bare existence, seeing no one, eating such food as came his way, and waiting in a numb and hopeless fashion for whatever would transpire.

The river made a great swing to westward and headed for the sea. Straight ahead was the setting sun, redder even than it had been in the morning, and bigger, a colossal plate of all-consuming fire apparently waiting for the world to come to it. It shone upon the water, making a dully glimmering path for the swan to glide along. But he was scarcely aware of such effects. His mind, having finished the contemplation of his life, was becoming a blank from having no longer anything to fix itself upon. He did not know how far the banks were now from the middle of the river where he was. In fact they were at some distance, and very low. Dreary flats stretched inland for miles, the drably even colour of the sick grass broken by twisting lines of creeks which filled with water only at the flood tide, each with a dozen rotting hulks hiding ashamedly within it. Here and there an haphazard scattering of ricketty jetties stuck out, some upstream and some down, abandoned, it seemed from their pitiful waiflike look, for centuries. This was a dismal landscape, depressing as the thoughts that came at evening to lonely men in strange towns.

The river was now very nearly at the end of its journey, and its pace though still insistent seemed to be slowing, as though, at the end of a long and busy day in the service of humanity, it were, a little sanctimoniously, tired. The swan it took no more note of than a man with other things to think of takes of the speck of dust that has lodged unirritatingly in the inner corner of his eye. And the swan, frail stately vessel on the flood of time, was scarcely more conscious of where he was, or what – a useless piece of flotsam dragged from the hinterland for disposal in the ocean's depths.

Once he had had the eagle's youth and lustiness – when he could not now recall and certainly it was of little consequence – who now, all but a carcase, was carried more swiftly than might be imagined to the sea.

Already he could smell the salt. A breeze was freshening the air; he could feel it on his brow, postponing the inevitable moment fast approaching when insensibility would overcome him. On the horizon the fiery sun was half submerged, and so strong was the impression of intense heat its colour gave it that it seemed the water must boil from this immersion. Land was out of sight now – out of anybody's sight, but still the current of the river was flowing smoothly and strongly, still bearing the swan implacably with it. The swan, though he did not know it, had been joined by other rubbish on this conveyor-belt; an empty cardboard carton, a deflated football, the rigid corpse of a diseased puppy, a crumpling elder bough, and sundry other articles of trash were all proceeding seaward at the same methodical speed, each one oblivious of the others.

Now at last he felt the first slight wave slap against his breast, and he knew the he had reached the open sea. How long would it be now? – how long would he drift before, one way or another, the end would come? The sun itself had disappeared, but the whole sky in front of him was glowing brilliantly red. It was as if the world were on fire. Never had he seen such a sky. He was thankful to have seen it before he died. – His death, he knew, was no longer imminent but actually upon him.

Then suddenly a feeling of unutterable peace came over him. He ceased to think of anything; there was no longer need to think. He felt as though from that burning sky arms were stretched out to welcome him, such ruthful all-comforting arms.

He beat his wings, rising transfigured from the water.

THE
TANAGER

As everyone knows, tanagers come in hundreds of varieties. Tanagers are very cliquy birds; the outsiders among them find it hard to become accepted by an established group.

There is a popular school of thought which blames this on their education, but that's only one of many causes. Those who belong to the same sporting or other clubs, those who come from the same part of the country, those who are members of the same religious group, above all those who share political opinions, all do the same thing. Any kind of common interest or affinity will serve to bind tanagers together; – it makes the newly encountered somehow into less of devils we don't know.

This seems to be reasonable. The only trouble is that those who don't have the links get excluded. But to cure it you would have not only to educate everyone at the same school (the same type of school wouldn't make sufficient difference in the long run: it would have to be actually the same school), but also to abolish all political parties and dissident religions and to make everyone have identical interests in life. Even then avine nature would find something to differ about.

So it looks as though the only answer is for all concerned to take good care that their affiliations don't make them exclusive.

THE
TEAL

The teal was something of a philosopher, and a matter which troubled him greatly was the question of exclusiveness. For, he felt, exclusiveness in the strict and pejorative sense is a negative quality and one to be avoided at all costs as the prime producer of loneliness. Yet exclusiveness in its derivative sense of taste and cultivation is an equally important positive quality, for it is on this that civilization is built.

THE
THRUSH

The thrush was a bore. She never stopped chattering for an instant. She was afraid that if she did the person she was talking to would take the opportunity to move off.

THE TICKBIRD

The tickbird doesn't look as though she has any life of her own. You never see her without her cow, either busily caring for it or trailing faithfully behind it as it moves from place to place. The impression she gives is that if the object of her singular devotion were removed there would no longer be any purpose in her life.

THE TOMTIT

A tomtit on the
windowsill gazing at the
company within.

THE
TOURACO

The touraco checked in resignedly. He had been stranded, and was forced to spend the night alone in a strange place.

First of all he endeavoured to get a message to his mate. That done, he examined his surroundings scrutinously, till he could have reproduced the detailed pattern of the wallpaper faultlessly, knew the precise whereabouts of every scratch on the furniture, and could recite the fire regulations by heart. Then he had a long slow wash. After that he wandered all along the corridors of the building, reading every notice several times with the utmost attention, and testing every chair in the public rooms. He managed to make that last until it was time for dinner. And dinner it was possible to spin out for more than an hour, by dint of forcing himself to eat with funereal incelerity. Afterwards, in spite of the rain, he tramped the dreary little town until he was tired enough to be confident of being able to sleep.

THE
TUI

He was an ineffectual old bird really, and he looked so pompous up there with his little white flaps stuck out aggressively. But there were some who remembered him for the inspiration they had got from a certain paragraph in one of his interminable sermons – one, as it happened, on the parable of the unrighteous steward. He said:

'I think there is also a lesson for us in spiritual philosophy in the story, and that is of the advisability of cutting one's losses. If things we set store by are taken from us, neither brooding, nor despair, nor nihilism, is the answer. Nor is continuing to fight battles which are recognizably and irretrievably lost. There is no future in the past. The only answer is to salvage what one can, make the best of it, and start again on that basis. Things often come right in the end. After all, there could have been no resurrection without the crucifixion.'

THE TURKEY

The Moss is a low, dark-soiled and rather apart place, which the main roads skirt and the sea mist sometimes obliterates. It is so flat that the farms which dot it stand out like volcanic islands in an empty ocean. They are self-contained and clearly separated from one another by the lands pertaining to them, fields of vegetables thriving in the peaty earth. The yards are neat, and turkeys strut at ease.

The farmers of the Moss might be lonely, but most of them are not. Only those who voluntarily shun the fellowship available sometimes feel cut off.

THE
TWELVE-WIRED BIRD
OF PARADISE

The distinction between being alive and being dead in the New Testament sense is not what we normally understand by life and death. We usually mean the difference between being animated and being inanimate, between breathing and not breathing. In the Christian sense the distinction between life and death is more like the difference between life and mere existence.

Thus when Paul talks about the wages of sin being death he doesn't mean that sinners are going to die in the physical sense. They are of course, but so is everybody else; that's not a punishment, that's part of life. What is meant is that sinners are not able to enjoy the fulness of life. That aphorism is part of the teaching on life and death (in the above sense) which Paul builds up for us throughout his letters. For Paul, as for Jesus, the hallmark of life is love = goodness + truth + service = knowledge of God, while death is simply this lack of the fulness of life.

Now life falls short of fulness through sin certainly, but equally through any form of hard-heartedness or self-centredness. Apart from that, the lives of many are less than full through no fault of their own. Their salvation is inextricably bound up with ours. That is where love comes in – an active, not a passive love. But 'good works' are not in themselves evidence of love. We can drive ourselves silly doing whatever it is we do do, however 'worthwhile'; if we do it for its own sake it isn't love, it's love that is necessary. To love is to live; to hate or to be indifferent is to be dead.

'Eternal life', said Jesus, 'consists in knowing God'. Do we know God? Are we alive or dead? We know nothing about any life hereafter, but whatever it is it can only be a projection of our life here and now. If we are alive in life we shall be alive in death; if we are dead in life, we shall be dead in death.

It is also very clear, surely, from the teaching of Jesus Christ, that life is to be enjoyed. Faith, hope, and love, are meant to add up to joy, not to an ecclesiastical platitude. You may remember the Noel Coward song about the middle-aged woman who (though she may have had a shallow idea of life) discovered, in the *nick* of time, that life is for living.

THE
URUBU

We vultures are all such ugly creatures. One can't help being aware of one's ugliness, and it seems to be a sort of barrier between us and others. What I can never make out, though, is whether our repulsiveness puts the others off or whether our fear that it does puts us off.

THE VIREO

About twenty years ago in a certain new world city there lived a certain clerk. He didn't come from that city. Indeed, hitherto he had had no connection with that city, or with anyone in it. So far as anyone knew, he just turned up there one day and happened to stay.

His dwelling was a small but pleasant room on the top floor of a large rooming house which had once been a prosperous private home. When I say a rooming house I mean that what was provided was a lockable furnished room with running water and a weekly change of linen. Meals you either had in a restaurant or cooked yourself on a two-plate electric burner.

The clerk worked in an insurance office in the business section of the city, twenty minutes' walk away. (That is to say it took *him* twenty minutes. Everyone else was so horrified at the idea of walking to work that one really can't say how long it would have taken them.) Every working day he left the house at twenty-one minutes to nine, and every working day he returned about six, having had his supper on the way. His lunch hour, after a quick couple of sandwiches in the drugstore next to the office, he would spend in briskly walking about the city. During the daylight hours of Saturdays he went for really long walks. Sundays, on the other hand, he mostly spent indoors.

He seemed a very ordinary sort of person really. He did his work efficiently and without bothering anyone. People at the office found him friendly enough, but never really got to know him. As to private life, so far as was known he had none.

Actually his private life consisted of three things. The first was his walks. These took him all over the city. But if anyone had been sufficiently interested to follow him, he would have observed that the clerk always (as though instinctively) stuck to residential streets, and that he was drawn to those of solid stone nineteenth-century continental appearance.

The second thing was a bird. This was a vireo, a small blue-headed chap, who often alighted on the broad dormer windowsill of his room. The two of them took no particular notice of each other. Nevertheless there seemed to be some kind of unspoken bond between them, as though each was glad of the other's existence.

And the third was a fixation the clerk had about a certain time and place. The time was the second half of the nineteenth century, and the place was the capital of a German kingdom (to which, incidentally, he had never been). He had a large collection of books about every aspect of that time and place, both pictorial and reading matter. He also had many gramophone records of the music which had emanated from it. Every evening with the aid of those books and records, and of a bottle of port, he would swiftly transport himself to that era and location of his choice, there to live vividly in an imaginary world until he fell asleep.

This was a world of cavalry parades and splendid uniforms, of women in bustles, of waltzes, of wine, of incense, of swordplay, of a divinely appointed king, of elaborate politeness, of everything that gave life colour. And he took this world with him into the streets. He could *see* the carriages. He could *hear* the words of command. He could *answer* the gay greeting thrown from a balcony.

Now to have a dream world to which to escape is fine. But as the months passed the dream world became more and more real to him, and the world of his insurance company and of radios and motor traffic more and more fantastic and remote. Increasingly often, in the office or the street, it was only with a shock of intense and amazed disappointment that he suddenly returned to an awareness of his actual surroundings.

It was not unnatural, therefore, that he should have a breakdown. He was ill for some time (quite how long he couldn't tell). One day when the fever had gone and he was lying awake, he knew all at once that he had to make a choice. He could embrace the dream world for good, but that meant death. Or he could choose life as it came in his own time and place; in that case he must renounce the dream world.

He had just about decided for the dream world, when he perceived the vireo standing inside the window regarding him, head atilt with enquiry. Quite unaccountably he all of a sudden plumped for life.

THE VULTURE

When the famine began there was a great comradeship in it; all
worked together to organize what supplies were available, and
shared what there was. But gradually, as things got worse, families
grew secretive and suspicious, clinging to whatever they could lay
hands on and casting envious eyes on whatever others secured.
The families grew smaller as the young and old and ill died. Then
those who had been healthy began to die, and by that time
individuals were not on speaking terms with one another, but gave
all their energies to scavenging. So, as they drifted towards their
own deaths, there was no one to care about it. In these
circumstances they felt that God had abandoned them.

THE WAXWING

The waxwing nodded to himself with self-approving sagacity (for
you have to mock yourself if you want to be taken seriously). Yes,
he thought, many birds have demonstrated that if a soul must
choose between the devil and loneliness the devil will nearly
always win.

THE WEAVER

Young Willie started work as soon as he was considered old enough to. He was looking forward to it. Knowing he was strong and active and quick-witted, he was convinced that he would be an excellent worker.

Arrived at the site, he was shown the section which he was to work on of the great communal nest that was being built. He started in right away. He fetched materials and placed them into position with a sure rhythm. He didn't hurry at all, merely worked at a natural pace; but since he had a gift for the work his pace was a little faster than most other birds'. And he felt like getting on with the job. Several others were plainly working more slowly than they need, but since it takes as much effort to work more slowly than is natural as it does to work more quickly, Willie couldn't see much point in that.

It was soon noticed that Willie's section was progressing so rapidly. One of the older birds strolled over to him and said (in quite a friendly way) the he should slow down or else everyone else would be expected to work as hard as he did. Now Willie's first thought (in the arrogance of his youth) was to reply that he'd work at his own pace and it was none of his business what others did. But he was new, and normally polite, and didn't want to cause trouble, so he just looked surprised and said, 'all right'.

For a while he did consciously slow his pace. But as the day wore on it became too much effort, and he slipped back into his natural speed. Another bird came across, this time not at all friendly, and ordered him to work slowly or he would be sent to coventry. Again he complied for as long as he remembered, and then automatically speeded up.

Then the word went round that he was not to be spoken to. Day after day he was avoided by his workmates. Whenever he approached they would turn and move away. If he opened his mouth there was dead silence. It takes a strong bird to stand up for long to having one's presence completely ignored. Then little accidents began to happen. The load he was carrying would be accidentally knocked out of his beak. His lunch would find itself trodden into the mud. His possessions would be unaccountably broken. The work he had done during the day would be taken to pieces during the night.

All this was most inhuman behaviour. But then of course those concerned weren't humans. What can be expected of birds?

THE WHINCHAT

Hour after hour, day after day, the flight went on. The precision of it was the remarkable thing: the steady beat of wings in unchanging rhythm, the sheer economy of movement. The whinchat scarcely understood the purpose of it, but purpose there must have been for there was never the slightest hesitation. Just steady, determined, flying. And fast. – In spite of the steadiness, the long confident strokes, the birds were moving through the air at tremendous speed, obeying some voice which evidently said: 'Keep flying'.

The scenery beneath them constantly changed (no time to investigate, the whinchat regretted fleetingly). Grey cities were succeeded by white, white by brown. Dark forests gave way to pale rounded hills, grassy plains to crags, fields of corn to the endless red desert. And still the flight went on relentlessly. Neither cold nor heat nor the driving rain had the slightest effect on it.

At times they paused for food. As though at a signal they swooped to the ground, alighted, fed themselves as silently and purposefully as they flew, and at another soundless unseen signal resumed the flight. At other times they paused for rest; they landed, slept where they stood, and suddenly took off.

'Keep flying'.

No sound was ever uttered, no gesture ever made. Nothing betrayed that they were aware of one another's existence, except that just occasionally in feeding one would brush against another and here would be a quick glance and a half smile. The whole fulness of relationship seemed to lie in the common effort and strength of purpose. The whinchat barely had time to find surprise that this came naturally to him, who had been the chattiest and bounciest of birds. The silence and discipline of this race towards whatever was their goal did not seem at all strange. Urgency was the keynote – the urgent prompting from within, 'Keep flying'.

They crossed the coastline now and headed out over the sea. This was a great stretch of ocean: no chance of food or rest, just flying, endless flying, without respite for days and nights on end. Flying till the wings ached and it seemed not another beat could be made. Flying till the head swam and nothing made sense any more. Flying like an automaton, without feeling, without reason, without the ability to do anything but just keep on, on, on, on, on.

After many days there was a different feeling in the air, a warm scent on the breeze that seemed to be promising of something. With the expectancy came a little relaxation. For the first time since leaving the land the whinchat was aware of the others, and turned his head to look at them. Suddenly he was thrilled, quite exalted, by a sense of achievement, and by a sense of companionship with these others with whom for weeks he had exchanged no ostensible communication. The terrible fatigue had vanished, and with a joy almost impossible to contain, the need for economy forgotten, he soared and swooped towards his destination.

THE
WHYDAH

The whydah had been instructed to draw up a series of questions for debate in a seminar on loneliness and politics, and these are what he constructed:

Is it true to say that two features of life in this age are a vast increase in 'political awareness' and an equally vast increase in loneliness?

Is there any immediate connection between these two things?

Or are they just facets of inevitable social change?

Is either increase right?

Is either increase necessary?

Is it true that civilization is collapsing?

Is this perhaps not so much a collapse of morals as of taste?

Is it not true to say that morals in practice are not all that different from in the past: it's just that there's no longer the taste to refrain from flaunting immorality?

Are we (presumably) speaking of morals in their broadest sense and not merely in any particular and perhaps rather perjorative sense such as absolute sexual continence?

(– In which last have they in any case ever actually existed?)

Are not morals properly speaking a matter of a sense of responsibility one to another in all relationships of every kind?

Isn't this simply the equivalent of love as applied to people we may not know?

For example, we don't steal from supermarkets, because that would be a failure in love towards persons unknown. But the question is, are those who do steal from supermarkets more shameless about it than in the past?

Has all this any connection with loneliness, either as a cause or as a result?

Are these questions reflected in the arts?

Have the arts become political?

(Were they not political in the past?)

Is this good or bad?
Is it true that expressionism is the mainspring of modern art?
Is it true that expressionism is another word for self-centredness?
Is it true that all art is expressionist?
Is expressionism the result of loneliness?

Is self-interest no longer respectable?
Is respectability no longer fashionable?
Is self-interest what politics are about?
Are not all polemicists in some fashion seeking an end to poverty
    and injustice?
Are they by their reforms imposing new injustices and a poverty
    of spirit?
Are they not seeking a social security for people, in the sense of
    abolishing the need to worry?
Are they bringing about a new social insecurity in the sense of a
    climate in which people are no longer secure in their social
    relationships?
Is a refusal to agree to differ proper enthusiasm or barbaric
    bigotry?
Is it a fact that there is little humour in most polemicists?
Does this contribute to polarization and hence to loneliness?

On the other hand is it not perhaps right to be earnest?
For is not the human soul a serious matter?
Are we justified in trusting it is the human soul polemicists are
    concerned about?
Are people in any way spiritually better off for being politically
    aware?
Is the knowledge of concern adequate compensation for increased
    loneliness?

Is it true that ideas have become more important than people?
(To clarify the point, is there an informative if irrelevant
    comparison with the unwritten doctrine of contiguity in the
    realm of political geography – that which turns imperialism
    from a vice into a virtue, 'colonialism' into 'consolidation',
    'freedom fighters' into 'separatist rebels', and 'oppression' into
    'security measures'?)
In other words, does each ideology have parallel jargons, one of
    approbation and one of opprobrium?
And does this contribute to separation?

Is it valid to speak of the loneliness of people separated by
politics?

Are people being driven more and more apart by the mutual
untouchability of party lines?

Loneliness being quite simply lack of communication, if people
lose the will to communicate won't loneliness become the
prevailing way of life?

THE
WIDOWBIRD

There were actually four of them, whose mates had all died round
about the same time.

Of the four, only Dora considered mating again, which in due
course she did. It was generally agreed that if she was really mating
for love this was an excellent thing, but if she was remating for the
sake of doing so, and in order to forget, then it was no answer at all,
and could only lead to comparisons and make matters far worse. In
the event she moved away with her new mate and lost touch, so no
one ever learned how it turned out.

Nora also moved away. Her health, poor thing, had been
undermined by the long hopeless illness of her mate, and when he
was finally allowed to die, that and her always slightly precarious
mental attitude proved insufficient to sustain her, though she tried
bravely. She decided to move, insisting that she would be much
better once she was away from old associations and memories. But
it didn't work out. Once out of reach of the support of old friends
and the way of life she had fashioned she very quickly went to
pieces.

Cora tried just the opposite; she lived as far as possible as though her mate were still alive. She was careful to do nothing he wouldn't have liked, kept all his possessions exactly as they were during his lifetime, and often spoke as though he would have to be consulted. She too was very brave, and fairly successful. But we all felt she would do better to accept the situation fully (and all were concerned, for she was a sweet old thing). She wasn't really trying to delude herself, we knew; she was just afraid to let altogether go of the anchor. The trouble is, unless you want to stay at a dead stop, anchors are such a drag.

Flora never forgot her mate either, but she used the memory in a different way. She had nursed him, not only physically but spiritually, gently through his painful dying to an easy death. The knowledge (completely without self-congratulation) that she had been able to make his death easy gave her some kind of rebirth, and she never showed the slightest sign of pining, though she certainly missed him dreadfully for the rest of her life. From then on she used tirelessly this gift she had discovered in herself. Whoever was in any kind of trouble or distress she would immediately visit. She knew instinctively exactly the thing to say to each one on each occasion. For those who'd lost loved ones, those who'd been crippled in accidents or acquired incurable diseases, those who'd been disappointed in one way or another, she would have just the right attitude, just the right remark. The number of creatures she saved from bitterness was prodigious. On especially poignant or difficult occasions she would leave exquisite letters, which were not only a comfort and inspiration at the time but a cherished treasure ever afterwards. She lived for many years, miraculously surviving several supposedly mortal illnesses.

THE WOODPECKER

There was a certain tree in the forest on which a number of woodpeckers were busy working together, all on excellent terms with one another. As it happened all but one of these woodpeckers were of the speckled type; there was one green one.

One day they were joined by a newcomer – speckled. He stared in astonishment at the green woodpecker. He nudged the other speckled ones with the tip of his wing.

'That is a green bird!' he hissed.

The others were puzzled. 'Why, yes, that is so', they said, and got on with their work.

'You don't understand', pursued the newcomer. 'He's, you know, *green*'.

The others stopped and looked at the green woodpecker. Of course he was green. What of that? They'd always known he was green but never considered it a matter worthy of comment. Some were green and some were speckled, and that was that.

But the newcomer insisted that green woodpeckers were different, and he went on and on dropping his poison into the other bird's minds. Eventually some of them believed him.

The green woodpecker couldn't help noticing that this was going on. Those who accepted the newcomer's view tried to avoid him, though they seldom actually insulted him. This gave him a feeling of isolation. Those who rejected such a view went out of their way to make a fuss of him; but this also, in view of the too obvious reason for it, tended to make him self-conscious, though he was immensely appreciative of their intention.

THE
WREN

Do you know Brecht's poem 'Seeräuber Jenny'? Jenny, the downtrodden maid in a sleazy hotel, dreams of the day when a pirate ship will arrive and attack the town, killing everyone in it except her, and the pirates will hail her as their leader and she'll sail away. The fantasy of a retarded teenager. But to my mind this is one of the greatest poems I know, because it captures exactly the mood of a child who feels rejected. I can remember having precisely such thoughts when I was a child. Later on in life one loses the nihilism of childhood. But also, unfortunately, one often loses the burning hope that is in the middle of childhood despair. Which is why adults who feel rejected often turn to suicide or drink or what-have-you.

THE
WRYNECK

'Also there is something more dangerous still, a stirring of youth, disappointed, aggrieved youth, which has never known the discipline of war. Imaginative and incalculable youth, which clamours for the moon and may not be content till it has damaged most of the street lamps'. Thus wrote John Buchan in 1935, in an otherwise undistinguished novel.
The wryneck was in a contemplative mood. The wrynecks, each in his own generation, had always been rebels in their young days. --

Which, he couldn't help feeling, was an excellent thing, for without rebellion complacency would become entrenched. And yet surely there had been times when the majority of birds found it possible to enjoy life for its own sake. Was there really no medium between complacency and discontent?

The truth was, he came to the conclusion, that bird is very lonely without a common cause. If God and King were no longer appropriate in this role, what could be? Vicarious football for a minority. But the more serious had to find a more serious cause. This cause was bound to be the discontent either of themselves or of others, and even if it was their own it would be that of others too.

If loneliness was to be the form of modern life, at least the wryneck was unable to be entirely depressed by this particular product of it.

THE XEMA

It had been airless and very hot for many days. Also there was a strange movement of the water beneath the surface; on top all seemed calm and smooth in keeping with the weather, but sudden violent eddies underneath would catch the ship from time to time, heeling her over or spinning her round, causing things to slide all over the place and throwing us against the bulkheads.

I don't know whether the sea and the breathless heat were the cause of it, but something was very wrong with the crew. Hardly a word could be spoken without a quarrel developing. Men went about sullenly, glowering at one another, avoiding the company of even their closest friends, their hands hovering towards their knives whenever an order was given.

A flock of birds had been following us now for days, fork-tailed gulls – xemas, they called them. They were greedy birds, and noisy; their harsh cries were a constant irritation. Gradually the men came to view these birds as the souce of their ills, as though they were evil spirits which would have to be exorcised before the sea and the weather and their own relationships could return to normal. They made themselves catapults and took shots at the birds, but with no success; they never hit one and they certainly didn't discourage them.

But then by some amazing chance one was caught alive. A particularly foul-mouthed elderly seaman was lying on the burning deck aft, when he just seemed to stretch out a hand and grab the bird. There was much savage exultation and discussion as to how to go about punishing the xema for the supposed sins of his fellows, and eventually it was decided to nail him by his wings to the roof of the deckhouse, doubtless to be pecked to death by the hungry others.

This was speedily done, but strangely enough he wasn't pecked by the others; they flew off, and we didn't see them again. The crew stood round shrieking and jeering like little children as the xema struggled frantically to release himself. The impression the bird gave of utter desolation, of a sense of having been abandoned by God and man, of pain and helplessness and unspeakable aloneness, affected me profoundly.

The bird soon died of course, and the carcase was thrown overboard. The men remained silent, but no longer apparently from sullenness and anger, rather perhaps from shame, as though they had been purified by the venting of their brutality, somehow redeemed, brought to a greater knowledge of themselves. Anyhow, before very long we ran into a breeze and a more predictable current, and life went on normally.

THE
XENOPS

The nest of a xenops is a tunnel dug into the ground. This particular xenops had dug his tunnel just inside the mouth of a long-disused silver mine, on the dry reddish hillside above a small and picturesque town. In the morning he crawled out of his tunnel and was suddenly confronted by the sunlight. For a moment this cheerful glare gave him the illusion that he was untroubled, but immediately the cloud would fall on his mind again.

For the xenops life was like having one's head perpetually in a blanket. No matter what he tried to do the shadow was there to spoil it. It was a memory that apparently nothing could remove. His upturned beak gave him a cheerful appearance which was horribly misleading. He was weighed down, almost crushed, by a load of guilt no one knew of; and because he was unable to speak to anyone about this he felt unable almost to speak to anyone about anything.

So he was aloof. As he made his way down the hill everyone smiled and greeted him in their usual fashion. He could twist out an acknowledgement, but nothing more, what would they think of him if they knew what he had not only been capable of but actually done? Or perhaps they did know and laughed at him behind his back, and their seemingly friendly smiles were in fact knowing and sarcastic. Yet really he knew that they didn't know and they wanted to be friendly, and that even if they did know most of them would still want to be friendly. But something in him refused to acknowledge this. He realised with a shock that he was on the verge of developing into a bitter and hateful creature.

He flew into the town and perched on a tree in the square in front of the church. He looked at the people. He watched them laughing over their coffee and pastries at the tables outside the café. He watched the loafers on the benches, asleep with grins on their faces and their big hats over their eyes. He watched the happily chattering girls carrying their bundles of laundry to the washing place. He watched the children chasing one another whooping round the square. He watched the fat shopkeepers with satisfied faces sitting on their doorsteps.

On an impulse he flew into the church. Here everything was in contrast with the noisy heat outside. It was cool, rather dim, and full of the sweet mysterious smell of incense, which contrived to be both comforting and inspiring. Direct sunlight came only through the windows of the octagonal wall supporting the dome, and fell on the retable. This was of immense height, entirely gilt, and carved with fantastic elaboration. Busts of saints, cherubs, horrid grimaces of driven devils, were all picked out in startling colour. This was fascinating to the xenops.

He stepped into the confessional. It was a long time before he could begin, but eventually, hesitatingly, he did. '"I confess to God almighty, to the Blessed Virgin Mary, to all the saints, and to you, Father, that I have sinned . . ."' He told of the injury he had done. When he had finished the priest spent many minutes digesting what the xenops had said, and then he spoke to him.

'What have you done to put things right?'

'Father, one of the parties is now dead . . .'

'Then pray for the repose of his soul. If you are truly repentant God will forgive you. There is nothing further for you to do with that. And the other party?'

'The other party is living, Father.'

'And what have you done about it?'

'Nothing.' The xenops scratched his head. 'You see, the injury was to some extent mutual. What I did to him was far worse than anything he did, but he began it and did me many petty hurts.'

'That makes it all the worse', said the priest, almost excitedly. 'That's how the devil operates, making gigantic snowballs from almost unnoticeable beginnings. Revenge is the saddest of all passions. Most of the evil in this world starts from somebody paying back – the philosophy of tit-for-tat. Never, never, return one injury for another. How can that possibly benefit anyone?' The priest was calmer again now. 'In *The Ladder of Perfection* we are reminded to regard even the smallest sin in ourselves as more serious and painful than the most atrocious sin in someone else. That is the attitude to have. You must go to the other fellow and must put things right as well as you can, but first of all you must forgive him freely for any wrong he may have done you.'

'But, Father, suppose he still doesn't forgive me?'

'That is beside the point. God's forgiveness of you depends on your forgiveness of the other fellow, not on the other fellow's forgiveness of you.'

The xenops shook his head. 'I cannot forgive till I feel myself to be forgiven. If the other fellow won't apologize first, then I must be assured of God's forgiveness before I can begin.'

The priest sighed. 'I can't absolve you on that basis. It's for you to unbend. Go. Read the Sermon on the Mount. Pray constantly for grace. When you can do what you have to, do it, and then come back to me.'

For many weeks the xenops refused to consider an apology. For many more weeks he considered it but couldn't bring himself to make it. It wasn't the thought of humbling himself that put him off, but an ashamedness which almost physically prevented him from having to do again with the one from whom he had parted in hate. But in the end he did all that could and ought to be done.

He presented himself in the confessional and repeated his previous confession. When the priest asked if he had put things right he told him what had been done. The priest spoke gravely and kindly.

'There is no occasion for further penance; you have done what is required. Advice you have had and taken; no doubt you will live by it in the future. "By the authority of Our Lord Jesus Christ committed to his Church I absolve you from all your sins ..."'

'Absolve'. 'Absolve.' 'Absolve'. The word rang in the xenops' head. 'I am absolved'. At last his spirit had emerged from the tunnel into the light of day.

THE
YARWHELP

Two thousand years ago Sedgemoor was much damper than it is now; in fact most of it was permanently under water. The Isle of Avalon, like other hillocks in the area, really was an island, and the rest of central Somerset was one with the Bristol Channel. Ships from Tyre would dock perhaps at Rodney Stoke, while cheerful Levantines paddled into Cheddar Gorge.

In those days the yarwhelps nested in their millions in the reed-beds and islets of Sedgemoor, just as they did more recently in the Fens, until thence too they were driven away by the drying out of the land. In those distant days yarwhelp was their only name; they hadn't earned the title 'godwit'.

Joseph of Arimathea used frequently to come on voyages to this part of the world. 'Joseph was a tinman' runs the old song, and indeed he dealt in tin and in lead and in all the other metals in which the Mendips were rich. Sometimes he would bring his teen-aged nephew Jesus with him on these trips. They would spend a few days in Priddy while Joseph saw to his business with the mine-owners, and Jesus would wander about and make friends with all and sundry in spite of the difficult language.

Once it happened that Joseph left Jesus in Priddy and arranged to meet him at the ship. By afternoon when Jesus said goodbye to his hosts the Mendip mist had come down thickly. He set off in the right direction and headed for the ship as best he could. Normally he would have been able to see it from the edge of the hills, but that day he could see nothing. He soon reached the sea, but didn't know whether to turn right or left.

He chose in fact to turn left, but after plodding along for some time assumed he must have chosen wrongly. By then, however, it was getting dark. He didn't think the ship would sail without him, or would sail in the fog at all, so decided the best thing to do was to find some shelter for the night. There was little hope of this down there by the water, and he was about to risk leaving it and trying to find his way to higher ground, when he tripped over some kind of low arbour of reeds.

He went round this construction on his knees until he found an entrance, and then crawled gently inside. He sensed that there was some kind of life in there, but couldn't tell what. But, grateful for the shelter, he lay there quietly and soon went to sleep.

When he woke up he found that he was both warm and dry. He opened his eyes and saw that daylight was filtering into the shelter. He noticed then that quite a few birds were gently staring at him. These, though unfamiliar to him, were in fact yarwhelps. He lay still a little while longer, and on thinking about it perceived that the birds had made room for him.

Very carefully he slid his way out. The morning was fine, wihout trace of mist, and he could see the ship in the distance. He looked at the place where he had spent the night and smiled.

'Happy is he that receives a stranger kindly', he said, 'for he shall know God.'

And that is how the yarwhelp came to be known as the 'godwit', or 'he who knows God.'

THE YELLOWHAMMER

Infinite millions of them rejoiced to eternity in the knowledge of one another's company. Where or when they died or had died made no difference. They belonged. Such is the communion of faithful yellowhammers.

THE YOKOHAMA

A high room. Perched near
the ceiling a fowl whose tail
   must not touch the floor.
Passivity. A servant
enters and bows. The bird sighs.

THE ZOSTEROPS

Let us, for the sake of argument, suppose that the zosterops is Melchizidek among birds. There is no virtue of himself. But when the Sacrifice is made, which is not his sacrifice but the Sacrifice, he is the focus and mouthpiece of the faithful for an eternal moment.

And, wherever and however and how few or many, equally that moment is the meeting point of the Deity and of the believing birds of all ages and all avinity.

The Author

Father David Drake-Brockman, born in 1933, was brought up in the U.K., India, Switzerland, and South Africa, and received his secondary education at Wellington College. After serving as a regular infantry officer in Germany, Korea, and Japan, he became first a shipping agent later a marine underwriter in Canada, then a schoolmaster in England. In 1968 he was ordained a priest. He has served in five dioceses, including Guyana and Polynesia, and is now a parish priest in Huddersfield.